Making the Early Years Foundation Stage work for you (0–36 months)

by

Helen M. Rowlands
and
Dr Hannah Mortimer

Acknowledgements
Staff at Hope Park Community Nursery, Liverpool
Busy Bees Childcare
Excerpts from *The Early Years Foundations Stage* (DfES, 2007)

A QEd Publication

Published in 2008

ISBN 978 1 898873 58 7

British Library Cataloguing
A catalogue record for this book is available from the British Library.

Published by QEd Publications, 39 Weeping Cross, Stafford ST17 0DG
Tel: 01785 620364
Website: www.qed.uk.com
Email: orders@qed.uk.com

Printed by Gutenberg Press, Malta.

Contents

Introduction

The Early Years Foundation Stage (DfES, 2007) provides support and guidance for those working with children aged between birth and 60+ months. This manual is intended to be used in conjunction with the framework for children under three and offers practical hints, tips and sample activities to help give you a real head start. Developed by Helen M. Rowlands and revised by Dr Hannah Mortimer, it draws on their experiences as a nursery nurse and educational psychologist respectively, and offers insights into how the framework was put into practice at Hope Park Community Nursery in Liverpool, where Helen had been nursery manager for more than 18 years.

In this introductory section a number of sample activities have been prepared to help individuals or groups get to grips with using this manual. These exercises will provide valuable training sessions in understanding how the framework really works and how to plan meaningful activities for the children in your care. The exercises have been tried and tested in many nursery settings and we feel confident that because of their very simplicity childcare staff will find them invaluable.

Throughout the section the ☞ symbol has been used to indicate a practical activity. Tick the box on the right when you have completed it to help you keep track of your progress.

Putting the manual into practice

Take some time to look through the manual and you will find that the core principles are the same throughout each section. There are sample activity sheets illustrating ways of applying each individual Focus of Development. At the end of each section there are blank activity sheets. In this introductory section you will be shown how to complete your own activity sheets and slot them into your planning. This means that there is no need for you to read slavishly through the entire manual, simply select the Area of Learning that you will be working with and focus on applying the framework to a child in that group. Once you are confident that you understand the implications with regards to that one child, transfer the framework to others in the age group. Once you have done this, and identified the differences inherent in the group, you should then look further and apply the same principles to another child from a different age group, or in a different Area of Learning. In this way you will find that everything slots into place very comfortably.

In order to simplify the use of gender, we have alternated fairly loosely between male and female throughout the manual.

Because it is usual that practitioners work alongside one or two others closely, as well as additional practitioners in neighbouring age groups, we suggest that introducing this method at a training session with your under threes team will have the most beneficial effect. We have continued in this section with a suggested outline for your workshop, but of course you may choose to follow this in isolation until you feel comfortable enough to continue.

Where to start?

As you are aware, the EYFS framework is separated into six **Areas of Learning**:

- Personal, Social and Emotional Development
- Communication, Language and Literacy
- Problem Solving, Reasoning and Numeracy
- Knowledge and Understanding of the World
- Physical Development
- Creative Development

This manual covers the typical age range of 0 to 36 months. A second book in this series focuses on 30 to 60+ months.

The EYFS is subdivided into typical (though flexible) age bands:

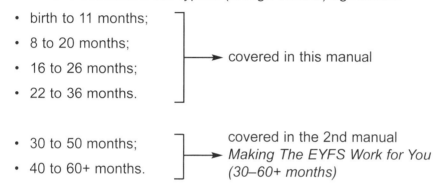

- birth to 11 months;
- 8 to 20 months;
- 16 to 26 months;
- 22 to 36 months.

> covered in this manual

- 30 to 50 months;
- 40 to 60+ months.

> covered in the 2nd manual
> *Making The EYFS Work for You*
> *(30–60+ months)*

Each Area of Learning is subdivided into various focuses of Development Matters (we abbreviate this throughout as Focus of Development) and these are listed at the start of each section, together with a simple coding system.

To ensure that our record-keeping and planning can be as simple as possible, this simple code has been allocated to each of the Areas of Learning and Focus of Development throughout the framework.

	Activity	Tick when completed
☞	In the manual, key areas of each of the focuses of Development are listed so take a little while now to familiarise yourself with the pages referring to Personal, Social and Emotional Development. There is no need at this point to go over the Sample Activity pages.	
☞	Once you have done this, photocopy page 6.	
☞	Gather together a pencil or crayon in each of six colours – purple, pink, green, blue, red and light brown. Collect a yellow highlighter too. Read 'A day in the life of Tilly Mint' and using your purple crayon *lightly* colour over the parts of Tilly's day that you feel reflect her Personal, Social and Emotional Development.	

A day in the life of Tilly Mint, aged 14 months

Time	Activity	Focus
8:00	Tilly arrives at nursery with her mum who passes over the terry towelling nappies. Tilly is happy to see her key person Sue and waves goodbye to mum easily. Sue helps Tilly build a house with the Mega Blocks.	
8:45	As the babies move through in to their own location, Tilly is holding Sue's hand, but pulling her through, keen to get to her own room. Sue sits Tilly down at the table, encouraging her to choose her own bib and try to put it on herself, offering a helping hand.	
9:00	Sheila brings in toast and jam for the morning snack and before the plates are ready Tilly is holding out her hand saying 'Ta' to Sarah who is nearest to the toast.	
9:30	While other staff tidy away the snack, Sue gets out a guitar that she has brought to nursery and Phil begins to play. Tilly is immediately interested in this and goes over to investigate. Phil shows her how to strum the strings and she is clearly impressed at the sounds she can make. Jeanette gets more musical instruments out and before long most of the group has joined in. Tilly goes from one instrument to another while she tries them out and ends up dancing for herself.	
10:45	After a brief interlude with a different selection of toys it is time for Tilly's group to visit the Sensory Room. She walks down the corridor by herself, leading the way to get there quicker. Phil is by her side but Tilly prefers not to hold her hand and walk under her own steam. In the Sensory Room, Sue selects the projected images of under the sea and Tilly enjoys following the moving images across the floor for more than 10 minutes, but then instantly dismisses them and runs around the room shouting loudly to hear her own voice. She plays independently with different equipment but stops regularly to check that she is still being watched and laughs when she knows that she has somebody's attention.	
11:15	Session over, it is time to walk back to the room for a nappy change and to get ready for lunch. Tilly is not quite so anxious to return and lags behind the group, eventually sitting down on the floor in protest at having to leave. Sue picks her up with a laugh to soften her thunderous expression and Tilly soon softens. Taking her straight into the nappy change Sue can sense that Tilly is getting tired and will need livening up if she is to enjoy dinner and pudding before falling asleep. Sue tickles her tummy and makes her laugh while getting her changed.	
11:30	Today's lunch is shepherd's pie with beetroot, which is brought in on plates to cool down. Again Tilly puts on her own bib and tries to get Phil's attention because she is nearest to the lunch. As soon as she has her plate in front of her, Tilly tucks in using her spoon and her fingers to push it on. When all of her group have their lunch Sue sits with them and asks if anybody would like her help. Asking Tilly directly, Tilly refuses to give Sue her spoon to help so Sue lets her get on with it. Watching her closely she offers more help as Tilly gets frustrated that she can't pick anything else up from the bowl. This time she lets Sue help her finish off her shepherd's pie. As her lunch bowl is collected by Jeanette, Tilly objects as Sue wipes her face and hands with a clean cloth in preparation for pudding which arrives almost instantly. Carrot cake is another of Tilly's favourites and she eats it very quickly.	

Time	Activity	Focus
12:10	After another wipe of her face and hands, Tilly is ready for her afternoon nap. Despite numerous attempts by Sue and other key staff, Tilly does not like to go to sleep on the floor cushions or in a cot. Instead she prefers to go to sleep in a buggy so Sue makes her comfortable, wheeling her up and down in the darkened room until she has dropped off. After a short while Tilly can be moved to a floor cushion where she will sleep longer than if she had stayed in the buggy. She is moved carefully, covered with her blanket and given her teddy to hug without her even batting an eyelid.	
1:45	Tilly sleeps longer than normal today and wakes in a very good mood. For a little while she is happy playing with the large wooden toys that have been set out but soon spots a group of older children playing outside. Going over to the door she bangs loudly, saying 'Out! Out!' to anybody who will listen.	
2:00	Phil brings in a small pile of coats belonging to the older babies and asks Tilly which is her coat. Tilly immediately identifies her coat and gives it to Phil to put on. As soon as her coat is on she stands impatiently at the door again shouting 'Out!' while she waits for the others in her group to have their coats put on. Door opens and she is raring to go. While outside she plays football, runs up and down the patio a great deal and bangs on the windows of other rooms to attract the attention of other children.	
2:30	Back inside she is ready for something calm so Phil asks her group 'Would you like a story?' Although she is not in Phil's group Tilly simply takes a seat with the group and enjoys *My Jungle* with the other group. Tilly thoroughly enjoys the book, making verbal comment about the pop-up animals and bright pictures. She remains sitting still while the book is read again, joining in slightly more than the first reading. After this Phil encourages the children to sit with their own books and they all sit happily and read the board books that they are given.	
3:00	Time for afternoon snack and Sheila has arrived with cheese and crackers. Without any instruction Tilly goes over to the table but finds no chairs. Instinctively she goes over to the milk kitchen and bangs at Sue, who she can see through the window. Sue gets the message and helps Tilly to put a chair at the table, asking her 'Where shall I put it? Do you want to sit by Andrew?' Tilly indicates where she would like to sit by pointing next to Jack and sits on the chair immediately. She enjoys her snack, needing no help at all, and almost helping Jack to finish off his before he spots her.	
3:30	After snack time there is a selection of coloured pencils and coloured paper laid out on the tables and Duplo on the floor. Tilly selects a handful of pencils and makes her marks on the paper with all of the pencils at the same time. Looking at her picture she is clearly pleased with her result and gathers a handful of pencils in the other hand too, making her marks on the paper with both hands at the same time. She gets fed up very quickly and drops the pencils, watching as some of them roll off the table and onto the floor. She sits playing with the Duplo, building a tower with Sue until her mum and dad arrive at 4:00.	
4:00	Sitting playing happily, for a minute or two Tilly is unaware that her parents have arrived. Sue smiles to them but does not draw Tilly's attention to them so that they can watch her play for a while. As soon as they are spotted any building plans are forgotten and she runs as far away as possible so that Dad has to chase her to put her coat on. This gives Mum a chance to ask Sue about her day, and Sue gives her lots of feedback before they leave for the afternoon.	

What next?

You may find that you have coloured in quite a lot of the text, but don't worry. Because the framework encompasses many of the ordinary but vital parts of a child's development it is natural that there will be some overlap.

Some of these examples might help you to check that you are on the right track:

- At 3:00pm Tilly indicates that she would rather sit by Jack than Andrew. This shows us clearly that Tilly can demonstrate her likes and dislikes included in the Personal, Social and Emotional Development Area of Learning

- At 12:10pm we can see that Tilly has clearly expressed her preference to sleep in her pushchair, but Sue has offered her recognition of this fact, ensuring that she feels accepted and comforted at sleep time.

- At 11:30am Tilly confidently manages to eat most of her lunch before taking up Sue's offer of help. Here she is demonstrating that she is clearly becoming confident in what she can do and is developing self-assurance.

- At 2:30pm Tilly is comfortable in joining in with another group at story time. She clearly demonstrates a sense of belonging to this extended group.

Once you are comfortable with your inclusions for Personal, Social and Emotional Development, move on to the other five Areas of Learning.

Take another look at 'A day in the life of Tilly Mint'. Can you see areas that overlap? If you can, this means that you are seeing the wider picture and looking at Tilly's development as a whole.

Sample activity pages

Take a look at the first sample activity page (on page 20) in the Personal, Social and Emotional Development section. This will help you use the activity pages in isolation (from the manual and the framework) and ensure that you have *all* of the key information to hand on just one piece of paper. You will recognise these headings:

- Area of Learning title.
- Focus of Development title.
- Age range.
- Development matters.
- Play and practical support.

What you will not be familiar with are the elements relating to the activity itself:

- Sample activity.
- Resources.
- Health and safety.
- Layout.
- Role of the key person.
- Note.
- Questions to ask/suggested interactions.
- Comments.

The sample activity is a means of reminding ourselves about the type of activity that might address the issues identified in the Area of Learning pages. They also serve as a really good reminder for those times when we feel that we need a little refresher when drawing up our plans.

In order to guide your session, as much information as possible has been included while at the same time keeping it manageable. For example, in the 'Recognising me' activity (page 21), we see this list in the 'Resources' section:

- Child-safe mirrors;
- Reflective surfaces;
- A key person with time for fun and quiet reflection.

We state these obvious facts to ensure that even the most inexperienced worker needs to remember that the mirrors selected must be child-safe and that this is a fun activity! We repeat the importance of this fact again in our 'Health and safety' section:

- Ensure that mirrors selected are appropriate for the age group and that freestanding mirrors are properly supported.

We do this again assuming that our activity may be carried out by the most novice practitioner and do not leave room for them to misinterpret our intentions.

In the 'Layout' section we give the practitioner more information about how we had seen our activity being carried out. Of course, you can be very specific when drawing up your own plans, listing your own equipment in your specific location.

The 'Role of the key person' section is, perhaps, the most important in ensuring that the activity is carried out as intended. Without careful thought given to the completion of this section, the activity may bear no relation to the one that you had planned. Here we provide this information for the key person:

- Sit quietly at the child's level and observe. Watch how they use things near to them and where their gaze strays to. Talk with them about what they see and about what they are doing. Encourage them to look at the mirrors in different ways, perhaps using the mirrors to direct the gaze of babies. Share the mirrors with them, encouraging them to look at their own face as well as your own or those of other children. Change the mirrors for different types intermittently, allowing exploration without allowing the child to become bored with the same activity. Use the mirrors to reinforce positive self-image even in very young babies, describing beautiful brown eyes or lovely curly hair, for example.

In one paragraph we are giving a practitioner a real insight into the activity, helping to ensure that this activity really *does* support the areas identified in Personal, Social and Emotional Development. Without this valuable information the practitioner may simply sit and let the baby play unsupported. What a different activity that would be!

To further reinforce the information provided in the framework, the 'Note' section is often taken from the 'Look, Listen and Note' sections of the EYFS. In 'Recognising Me' the practitioner is asked to:

- Note how babies use the opportunities you provide, to develop, show and communicate their preferences and decisions.

It is intended that practitioners use these notes as prompts for taking notes to add to each child's developmental files. When writing up your own activity planner you may prefer to note down a very specific request for a specific child or group of children.

To further support the 'Role of the key person' section there are questions to ask or suggested interactions. Only one or two ideas are suggested, but the intention is to highlight the fact that he/she *should* be interacting with the children, whatever their age. I am sure we have all witnessed nursery staff setting out an activity and then taking a back seat while the children play. Prompting practitioners to ask questions or to interact reminds them that their job is not finished once the equipment is set up, but often, more importantly, offers another link between the activity and the Area of Learning/Focus of Development it is intended to address.

The questions 'Who can you see in the mirror?', 'Where's James?' and 'Where's James's nose?' are intended to set James thinking about who he can actually see and also what specifically he is looking at.

Next is a 'Comments' box. Throughout the manual this has been used for two different types of comment. In this example it has been completed as if the box had been left blank at the start of the activity and the practitioner had updated it with the following information:

- This was a very relaxing and enjoyable session that would definitely benefit from repeat sessions. More could have been achieved with a larger variety of mirrors, so will borrow more mirrors from other rooms for the next session.

This comment is very helpful to the next practitioner carrying out this activity and, of course, serves as a very valuable tool for demonstrating that we evaluate our sessions as a matter of course.

There are occasions where the 'Comments' box is used to serve as a reminder to the practitioner about certain matters. In the 'Peek-a-boo' activity (page 29), the comment reads:

- Try to play this right the way across the room to encourage a feeling of security that does not rely on proximity.

When drawing up your own activity planners you must decide which is appropriate for each planner, but remember to make a note of evaluative comments on the additional page so that other practitioners will benefit from your thoughts and, of course, that further sessions can take your thoughts into consideration before beginning.

Drawing up your own activity planner

If you are working through this section as part of a team meeting you might like to split up into groups for this next activity. It is recommended that you all choose the same activity to draw up though, as this will serve to highlight the differences and, of course, the importance of noting down exactly what you had intended from the very beginning.

	Activity	Tick when completed
☞	At the back of each section you will find a blank activity planner. Start by photocopying these for you to practise on.	
☞	Because we need to make a start somewhere, go to your planner for next week and choose the activity scheduled for Monday morning.	
☞	Starting at the 'Sample activity' row, take your time and complete the form up to and including the 'Questions to ask' box.	
☞	Once completed, take a good look at the activity you have drawn up and then spend some time thinking about where this activity would best fit into the framework. When you are happy with this, move on to complete the Area of Learning.	
☞	Look at it further before completing the Focus of Development as occasionally the most obvious is not the most appropriate.	
☞	Once you have done this go to the appropriate page in this manual that outlines the Development Matters focus in more detail. Highlight the 'Development matters' section and enter this into your table exactly as it is written. Remember that these sheets may be used in isolation from the framework and/or this manual so we need to have all of the important information with us.	
☞	Before you enter the 'Play and practical support' section into your table, consider any amendments that you might like to make to suit your setting. Do this now.	
☞	Finally, look once more at your completed table. Would your activity benefit from additional notes in the 'Comments' section? Remember that leaving this section blank is perfectly acceptable, but only *if* there are no additional comments for you to make.	
☞	If you have split into several groups for this activity you should feed back to each other now. It is important that everybody is comfortable before moving on to the next exercise.	

Hopefully you can now see why we started with this activity. Being able to complete the table for activities that we already have planned will be helpful when it is time to implement this new planning system. Before long, though, you will need to plan from scratch, so then would be a good time to plan from a different perspective. Let us take some time now to plan directly for Areas and Focuses of Development, and identify activities that support their requirements.

	Activity	Tick when completed
☞	Return to the same groups, but this time select different Areas to plan for. If you have four groups you could suggest that you select activities as follows:	
	Group 1 ⟶ Communication, Language and Literacy ⟶ Language for Communication	
	Group 2 ⟶ Problem Solving, Reasoning and Numeracy ⟶ Calculating	
	Group 3 ⟶ Knowledge and Understanding of the World ⟶ Exploration and Investigation	
	Group 4 ⟶ Physical Development ⟶ Movement and Space	
	This time start by completing the table from the top down, referring to the Focuses of Development pages for confirmation of the requirements for the activity.	

	Activity	Tick when completed
☞	Now feed back to each other. Remember that each group needs to *inform* the others about exactly how and why the activity meets the requirements of the Areas of Learning.	

Remember at this stage to remind everybody to be open to questioning. We all need to be comfortable that we understand what we are doing before we move on to the next section. Take some time to see each of the activities planned with a child in mind from that age group. Does it fit? Are there alterations to be made now that you can see a specific child in the activity? Are there alterations to be made if you give the planner to a certain practitioner? Will your descriptions need to be clearer, or the health and safety section more prescriptive? Of course, only you decide that, but remember to ask yourself those questions regularly.

There is one more exercise before we can discuss fitting our activity planners into our schedule. Think about an activity such as sand play. Of course, playing in the sand involves 'Designing and Making'. Or is it 'Exploring Media and Materials'? Perhaps it is 'Shape, Space and Measures' or 'Self-Confidence and Self-Esteem'? Well actually it could be all of these things. The key here is to identify clearly the Focus of Development that you are working towards and make sure that your 'Role of the key person' and 'Questions' are addressed accordingly.

	Activity	Tick when completed
☞	For the final exercise in this section return to the same groups and select a different Area of Learning and Focus of Development completely at random and ask the groups to plan a sand activity that fits. Take only 5 minutes for this exercise as it is the realisation that we can do this that is the point, rather than the plans themselves that matter.	

Although sometimes we might identify just one small aspect of the play that is relevant, we can make sand play fit into *any* of the Focuses of Development listed. Imagine how useful this is for a child who is only comfortable at one or two activities and needs a little support to become comfortable with different situations. In future meetings you might want to review this and choose a different activity to fit into each of the Focuses of Development.

Using the framework to support your teams

Looking closely at our 'Day in the life of Tilly Mint' you will see how often the unplanned parts of Tilly's day can be included when assessing her development. We saw Focuses of Development covered as she arrived in the morning and went home at the end of the day. More are addressed at meal times, nappy changes and even putting on coats to go out to play. Of course, we know that these things count as areas of development, but how often do we remember to record them?

	Activity	Tick when completed
☞	Take some time to look through her day and with a yellow highlighter go over unplanned events that can be recorded in Tilly's Tracker (or developmental chart).	

By doing this you will have drawn up a list of activities or events that are covered by the framework but that need no, or very little, planning on your part. You will, of course, need to remember to record them and remind all practitioners that these events are important.

Once this is completed you will then have a long list of areas that are not likely to be covered unless you include them in your plans. This will probably include art and craft activities, music, story times and physical challenges among others.

Take another look at your planner for next week. It may look a little like this:

Monday	Tuesday	Wednesday	Thursday	Friday
Shredded paper play	Gloop	Baby assault course challenge	Washing ourselves	Push-along toys
Making music from everyday objects	Recognising me	A tactile collage	Taste tests	A very messy painting activity

It certainly looks very interesting. Making a mess is great fun if it is for a purpose. In order to make this a more purposeful planner, what we need are some *focuses*. Using a baby room as an example, we have 12 babies under 18 months, cared for by four practitioners. Of course, these babies do not fall easily into equal divisions according to the framework, so we need to plan our activities to suit the children expected for each individual session. Each key person can identify the focuses of development she has planned for her group of children. For example, Sue's planner might look like this when she has clearly identified what she is going to focus on:

Monday	Tuesday	Wednesday	Thursday	Friday
Shredded paper play **PSED 3**	Gloop **CLL 5**	Baby assault course challenge **KUW 3**	Washing ourselves **PSED 5**	Push-along toys **KUW 2**
Making music from everyday objects **CLL 3**	Recognising me **PSED 1**	A tactile collage **CD 2**	Taste tests **KUW 4**	A very messy painting activity **PD 3**

Sue has planned for the following Focuses of Development:

PSED 1	Dispositions and Attitudes	**CLL 3**	Linking Sounds and Letters
PSED 3	Making Relationships	**CLL 5**	Writing
PSED 5	Self-Care	**PD 3**	Using Equipment and Materials
KUW 2	Designing and Making	**CD 2**	Exploring Media and Materials
KUW 4	Time		

Sue will know the abilities of her group and will be conversant with *Trackers 0-5* (see bottom of page 15 for more details) for each of her children, and will work towards reinforcing areas from these Focuses of Development where her support is needed.

Later on in the year, as the children in her group have developed, we might see her planning activities in a higher age-range or looking for progression into other Areas of Learning and Focuses of Development.

Use a similar grid on a large piece of paper to record your unplanned events. Every now and again, when you see a Focus of Development covered spontaneously, note down the appropriate code with the child's name on a Post-it note. Stick this on to the grid for later recording. For Tilly Mint you might see the following focuses recorded:

Monday	Tuesday	Wednesday	Thursday	Friday
Peek-a-boo PSED 3	Welcome to nursery CLL 4	Can you find ...? PD 1	Making choices at snack time KUW 6	What happens if you watch me paint? CD 2
Cardboard box play PD 3	Making music from everyday objects CLL 3	Getting ready for a nap KUW 4	Whose coat is this? PSED 5	What's in this box? PSRN 2

Using the activity planners for the first time

Look again at your planner for next week. You will probably have at least ten core activities listed, possibly more. Don't panic. It is unlikely that you will have time to plan each of these activities now, but stop and think. We have already made a start on some of these activities in our earlier exercises and as long as you are happy with the results you can start using them straight away.

Having completed these exercises in your training session you should feel comfortable completing the activity planners as you go along and it is recommended that you try to have two written up each day. It will take a few weeks to cover all of your main activities, but also during this time try to encourage your team to write up one or two spontaneous events each week. Of course, you can take turns with other members of the team so that the task does not become too much of a chore, but consider how much more confident individuals will feel in an Ofsted inspection when they can demonstrate their detailed plans to an inspector *and* the recording of spontaneous activities as well!

Monitoring your progress

It is important to remind ourselves that the completion of the activity sheet is not the end product. Each time the activity has been carried out the practitioner will need to add dated comments to the second sheet to inform others of their findings. You can, of course, copy as many of these as you may need to ensure that evaluation and assessment is working to your advantage. By monitoring activities as we go along we are demonstrating a commitment to keeping our plans up to date and using the most recent assessments to the benefit of the children in our care.

Let us look once more at Tilly Mint. We have built up a picture of her making progress across all of the six Areas of Learning and Development – yet Tilly is just 14 months old. What are we to do to ensure that Tilly continues to develop into a confident and competent child? For Tilly it will be important that we watch her progress closely for a short period of time. Pay special attention to any gaps identified and watch for any areas that are identified strengths or weaknesses. Imagine, for example, that Tilly was doing so well that she really needed more additional challenges in this area to prevent her becoming bored and frustrated. All we need to do is look for the next age range and move on. There is no need to be bound by age restrictions. The ages are there simply because in most cases they are appropriate. In some they are not. Remember that this can work both ways and it may also be helpful with some children to look to pages in earlier sections for support.

Over a period of a few weeks you will be able to see a picture developing of some familiar Focuses of Development reoccurring regularly throughout your planners. What you may not spot easily are those that are regularly overlooked. You will need to develop your own system to help you spot these, but one of the most efficient ways of identifying gaps in your planning is to complete a regular 'A day in the life of …' for the children in your group, as demonstrated with Tilly Mint. If each of your key people takes more detailed notes for just one day each week and writes/types them up in a similar fashion to Tilly's day, you can demonstrate that not only are you assessing your practice overall, but you are also assessing it more closely in relation to individual children. An added bonus is that your parents and carers will love this detailed record of their child's day, which of course can be adjusted to suit your own needs. If you have somebody with good IT skills you could include digital photographs in your table, showing the child painting, sleeping, eating etc. Save each of these in a loose-leaf file and before long you will have a fantastic record of evidence for use in Ofsted inspections, parents' evenings, open days or any other opportunity to show off the children's progress.

There are examples of how to use your case studies to record progress at the end of the manual.

Summary

By the time you have completed all of the exercises in this book and worked with the system for a month or so you will be able to:

- identify and plan for each of your under three age ranges according to the *EYFS* framework;

- draw up specific activity planners to guide and support the practitioners in your team;

- make additional comments each time the activity is carried out to keep other practitioners informed;

- record spontaneous events in a similar format;

- evaluate your planning;

- further identify gaps to be addressed in your children's development by transferring observations made to developmental Trackers*.

And finally

To make this manual a *real* success for your under threes team it will be important to remember that this should be a working document. Make comments about questions raised, lessons learned or even nightmare activities that should *never* be repeated unless we take a number of precautions first.

*The Trackers referred to here are those published by QEd Publications (contact details at the front of the book). *Trackers 0–5: Tracking children's progress through the Early Years Foundation Stage is a* simple and effective way of monitoring progress.

Summary of codes used

Personal, Social and Emotional Development

PSED 1	Dispositions and Attitudes
PSED 2	Self-confidence and Self-Esteem
PSED 3	Making Relationships
PSED 4	Behaviour and Self-Control
PSED 5	Self-care
PSED 6	Sense of Community

Communication, language and Literacy

CLL 1	Language for Communication
CLL 2	Language for Thinking
CLL 3	Linking Sounds and Letters
CLL 4	Reading
CLL 5	Writing
CLL 6	Handwriting

Problem Solving, Reasoning and Numeracy

PSRN 1	Numbers as Labels and for Counting
PSRN 2	Calculating
PSRN 3	Shape, Space and Measures

Knowledge and Understanding of the World

KUW 1	Exploration and Investigation
KUW 2	Designing and Making
KUW 3	ICT
KUW 4	Time
KUW 5	Place
KUW 6	Communities

Physical Development

PD 1	Movement and Space
PD 2	Health and Bodily Awareness
PD 3	Using Equipment and Materials

Creative Development

CD 1	Being Creative – Responding to Experiences, Expressing and Communicating Ideas
CD 2	Exploring Media and Materials
CD 3	Creating Music and Dance
CD 4	Developing Imagination and Imaginative Play

Personal, Social and Emotional Development

(0–36 months)

Personal, Social and Emotional Development
(0–36 months)

Section index

Selection of Sample Activities

		Birth – 11 months	8 – 20 months	16 – 26 months	22 – 36 months
PSED 1	Dispositions and Attitudes	Page 20	Page 21		Page 22
PSED 2	Self-confidence and Self-esteem	Page 24	Page 25		Page 26
PSED 3	Making Relationships	Page 28	Page 29	Page 30	
PSED 4	Behaviour and Self-Control	Page 32			Page 33
PSED 5	Self-care		Page 35		Page 36
PSED 6	Sense of Community			Page 38	Page 39

A blank planner for you to copy and complete for the children is on page 40.

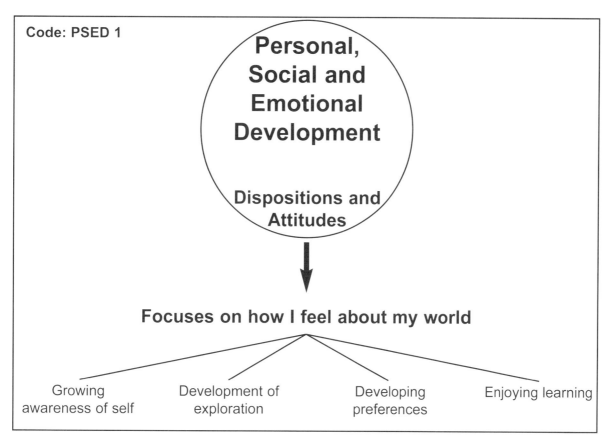

Code: PSED 1

Personal, Social and Emotional Development

Dispositions and Attitudes

Focuses on how I feel about my world

Growing awareness of self   Development of exploration   Developing preferences   Enjoying learning

Development Matters

Birth – 11 months
- Develop an understanding and awareness of themselves.
- Learn that they have influence on and are influenced by others.
- Learn that experiences can be shared.

8 – 20 months
- Become aware of themselves as separate from others.
- Discover more about what they like and dislike.
- Have a strong exploratory impulse.
- Explore the environment with interest.

16 – 26 months
- Learn that they are special through the responses of adults to individual differences and similarities.
- Develop a curiosity about things and processes.
- Take pleasure in learning new skills.

22 – 36 months
- Show their particular characteristics, preferences and interests.
- Begin to develop self-confidence and a belief in themselves.

You will find suggestions for *Look, listen and note*, *Effective practice* and *Planning and resourcing* in the EYFS Practice Guidance.

Personal, Social and Emotional Development

Personal, Social and Emotional Development
Dispositions and Attitudes (Birth – 11 months)

Development matters	Play and practical support
Develop an understanding and awareness of themselves. Learn that they have influence on and are influenced by others.	Playfully imitate young babies, giving them full eye contact, interacting with their playthings, watching the ways they use them and showing them new things to do.

Sample activity	Toys with movement.
Resources	Gather together a selection of toys that make movement but don't move away – spinning tops, dancing teddies etc.
Health and safety	Ensure that the baby does not topple forward onto a toy that may hurt her.
Layout	Sit the young baby carefully propped up with lots of soft cushions so that she can move safely. Arrange a selection of the toys within sight of the young baby and sit facing her.
The role of the key person	Take your lead from the young baby's gaze and watch how she reacts when you set one of the toys off. Encourage her to help set it off again, using her own hand to push the top down. Maintaining full eye contact keep her interest by encouraging participation, moving on to the next toy as her attention decreases. Return to favourite toys intermittently, aiming to extend her interaction with the toy.
Note	Note how young babies begin to explore their body's movements and the environment in individual ways.
Questions to ask/ suggested interactions	• Can you reach this spinning top? • Can you push your hand down to make it go again? • Shall we try another toy? • Which one would you like?
Comments	Make notes of her favourite toys and those that don't go down too well. Also note where progress is made with extended reach or imitating your actions to set the toy off.

Personal, Social and Emotional Development

Personal, Social and Emotional Development
Dispositions and Attitudes (8 – 20 months)

Development matters	Play and practical support
Become aware of themselves as separate from others.	Provide a variety of mirrors in different places to help babies explore what they look like and who they are.

Sample activity	Recognising me!
Resources	Child-safe mirrors, reflective surfaces, and a key person with time for fun and quiet reflection.
Health and safety	Ensure that mirrors selected are appropriate for the age group and that freestanding mirrors are properly supported.
Layout	Prepare the room/area with mirrors and reflective surfaces of many different types – freestanding mirrors that we can see behind, mirrors to hold, large mirrors to see both of our faces at the same time, mirrors we can walk towards, lie underneath and mirrors that we can cover with sheet for peek-a-boo play.
The role of the key person	Sit quietly at the child's level and observe. Watch how they use things near to them and where their gaze strays to. Talk with them about what they see and about what they are doing. Encourage them to look at the mirrors in different ways, perhaps using the mirrors to direct the gaze of babies. Share the mirrors with them, encouraging them to look at their own face as well as your own or those of other children. Change the mirrors for different types intermittently, allowing exploration without allowing the child to become bored with the same activity. Use the mirrors to reinforce positive self-image even in very young babies, describing beautiful brown eyes or lovely curly hair, for example.
Note	Note how babies use the opportunities you provide, to develop, show and communicate their preferences and decisions.
Questions to ask/ suggested interactions	<ul><li>Who can you see in the mirror?</li><li>Where's James?</li><li>Where's James's nose?</li></ul>
Comments	This was a very relaxing and enjoyable session that would definitely benefit from repeat sessions. More could have been achieved with a larger variety of mirrors, so will borrow more mirrors from other rooms for the next session.

Personal, Social and Emotional Development

Personal, Social and Emotional Development
Dispositions and Attitudes (22 – 36 months)

Development matters	Play and practical support
Show their particular characteristics, preferences and interests.	Let children make decisions about how and where to display their paintings or allow them to select which toys to play with or who to sit with.

Sample activity	Displaying a piece of free painting.
Resources	Equipment to carry out a piece of artwork. A selection of materials to back the finished result and a number of places to display it.
Health and safety	Ensure that all backing and fixing materials are appropriate to the age of children participating, providing adult support where staplers might be needed.
Layout	Lay out a selection of backing materials near to the painting corner.
The role of the key person	Observe children painting and respond when a child seems particularly pleased with the finished article. Talk with them about their painting and ask them if they would like to put their picture up on the wall, either at nursery or at home. Ask the child if they would like you to help them back the picture once it has dried, and encourage them to select an appropriate selection of papers. Try to ensure that this is the child's work and that *you* are helping *them* to back their own picture, not worrying if it is not displayed straight unless the child wants it straight. Once backed, talk with the child about spaces available for it to be displayed, pointing out that it cannot be on top of another child's work.
Note	Note how children explore, play, socialise and make sense of their experiences.
Questions to ask/ suggested interactions	• Are there any colours in your picture that you would like to use in the backing? • Would you like to put the Blu-tack on or shall I? • Where do you think your picture would look best?
Comments	Care should be taken that pictures are not displayed on top of each other. Also bear in mind the nursery budget and only offer the children materials that you are happy using for this purpose. Expensive shiny card will look lovely as a backing, but you won't be popular with others if you use it all up in this way.

Personal, Social and Emotional Development

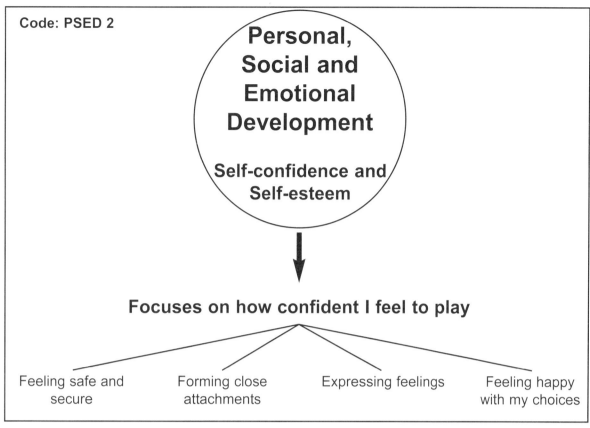

Code: PSED 2

Personal, Social and Emotional Development

Self-confidence and Self-esteem

Focuses on how confident I feel to play

Feeling safe and secure   Forming close attachments   Expressing feelings   Feeling happy with my choices

Development Matters

Birth – 11 months
- Seek to be looked at and approved of.
- Find comfort in touch and in the human face.
- Thrive when their emotional needs are met.
- Gain physical, psychological and emotional comfort from 'snuggling in'.

8 – 20 months
- Feel safe and secure within healthy relationships with key people.
- Sustain healthy emotional attachments through familiar, trusting, safe and secure relationships.
- Express their feelings within warm, mutual, affirmative relationships.

16 – 26 months
- Make choices that involve challenge, when adults ensure their safety.
- Explore from the security of a close relationship with a caring and responsive adult.
- Develop confidence in own abilities.

22 – 36 months
- Begin to be assertive and self-assured when others have realistic expectations of their competence.
- Begin to recognise danger and know who to turn to for help.
- Feel pride in their own achievements.

You will find suggestions for *Look, listen and note*, *Effective practice* and *Planning and resourcing* in the EYFS Practice Guidance.

Personal, Social and Emotional Development

Personal, Social and Emotional Development
Self-confidence and Self-esteem (Birth – 11 months)

Code: PSED 2

Development matters	Play and practical support
Seek to be looked at and approved of. Find comfort in touch and in the human face.	Find time to play, have fun, sing and laugh with young babies.

Sample activity	**Let's all join in with nursery rhymes!**
Resources	No resources required at all … unless you want to extend your range of nursery rhymes and sing along with a children's CD.
Health and safety	There are no health and safety risks to this activity.
Layout	Sit or lie all of the children in a circle in a comfortable position.
The role of the key person	Sitting at the same level as the young babies, maintain a contact with one or two of the group throughout, making sure that there are enough staff to incorporate all of the group meaningfully. Select a small repertoire of songs with a tactile feel, perhaps starting with a song that welcomes everybody into the session. 'Hello, Holly Richardson, and how are you?', repeated for each of the participating young babies and shaking each of their hands as you sing their name offers great opportunities for eye-to-eye contact, physical contact and name recognition. Moving on to different songs, the key person can move the young baby's hands to touch her head, shoulders, knees and toes, building up the fun element as the speed increases. Other movement songs such as 'Wind my bobbin up' allow for similar fun.
Note	Remember to agree on tunes beforehand if more than one exists for a particular song. Select a small number of songs to sing regularly, returning to the same ones often. Introduce new ones sparingly, but intermingled with old favourites.
Questions to ask/ suggested interactions	• Did you enjoy that one, Holly? • Shall we sing 'Wheels on the bus' now? • Can Holly clap her hands?
Comments	Remember to include all of the young babies in the introductory session, repeating it if others arrive to join your group. Try not to use too many different songs over a short period, but do try to make your selection varied.

Personal, Social and Emotional Development

Personal, Social and Emotional Development
Self-confidence and Self-esteem (8 – 20 months)

Development matters	Play and practical support
Feel safe and secure within healthy relationships with key people.	Increase the time babies play independently, remembering it is comforting for them to hear familiar sounds and have you near.

Sample activity	What can we find?
Resources	A box of safe bits and pieces – assorted different bits of toys or teddies etc.
Health and safety	Ensure that items in the box are appropriate to the child's age. Watch carefully to ensure that the box does not topple or the baby does not fall into the box.
Layout	Set the box out on a clear space on the floor and sit alongside it.
The role of the key person	Sit quietly, looking carefully and rummaging in the box. As you get the attention of one or two babies ask them if they would like to join you, inviting all who pay attention. Encourage them to look for what they can find in the box, but as they begin to enjoy themselves sit to one side and leave them to it. As individual babies look to you for attention respond positively and verbally, but stay at a distance to encourage independent exploration to continue. Ensure that toys discarded by one child are carefully replaced back in the box for others to enjoy, but without interfering. Watch closely to prevent quarrels, distracting individuals away from a fought after toy.
Note	Note how babies become confident in exploring what they can do with less dependence on adults.
Questions to ask/ suggested interactions	• What can we see in this box? • Can Andrew find the blue teddy? • Shall we let Alex play with that shell while we look for the car?
Comments	It might be sensible to start this activity in a separate room with a few select children, selected in order to avoid fighting over popular items. Take care not to participate more than is necessary, withdrawing participation further with repeated activities. Remember that the same box of toys will not encourage individual exploration each time. Deliberately use different toys, different boxes and different times of the day to encourage further exploration.

Personal, Social and Emotional Development

Personal, Social and Emotional Development
Self-confidence and Self-esteem (22 – 36 months)

Development matters	Play and practical support
Begin to be assertive and self-assured when others have realistic expectations of their competence.	Provide dressing up clothes and materials that help children find out what it feels like to be someone else.

Sample activity	**Getting to know our persona doll.**
Resources	A doll (or puppet) with a clearly defined persona and life history that is familiar to the children. A familiar worker to share the discussion with the children.
Health and safety	There are no health and safety risks to this activity.
Layout	Sitting in a circle with the persona doll clearly visible to all.
The role of the key person	Identify a recent experience that upset one of your group and use this as a basis for your story about your persona doll called Joe. Start the session by reminding the children about Joe's story and then tell the group that Joe was upset the other day when somebody snatched his toy and wouldn't give it him back. Encourage the children to empathise and tell you how they would feel if somebody did that to them. Ask the children what they might do if somebody did that to them and offer a suggestion from Joe that you feel might be the best answer. Also ask the children to consider what they might do if they saw somebody being unkind to somebody else and again respond with Joe's thoughts. Remember to close the session on a positive with lots of hugs for Joe and each other.
Note	Note how you ensure that each child is recognised as a valuable contributor to the group and how you celebrate cultural, religious and ethnic experiences.
Questions to ask/ suggested interactions	• Why do you think Joe felt upset? • What could you do to help him? • Why do you think Asham took Joe's toy?
Comments	Remember to use your persona doll for fun and positive experiences otherwise the children might begin to associate his visits with a lecture. If you do not have an official persona doll, there is no problem with you identifying another doll to take on this role. Try to ensure that its life history is agreed with all workers beforehand as any conflicts in stories from one worker to another *will* be picked up by the children.

Personal, Social and Emotional Development

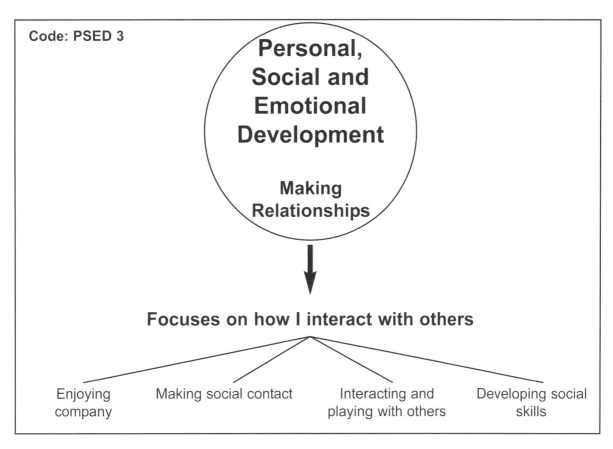

Code: PSED 3

Personal, Social and Emotional Development

Making Relationships

Focuses on how I interact with others

| Enjoying company | Making social contact | Interacting and playing with others | Developing social skills |

Development Matters

Birth – 11 months
- Enjoy the company of others and are sociable from birth.
- Depend on close attachments with a special person within their setting.
- Learn by interacting with others.

8 – 20 months
- Seek to gain attention in a variety of ways, drawing others into social interaction.
- Use their developing physical skills to make social contact.
- Build relationships with special people.

16 – 26 months
- Look to others for responses which confirm, contribute to, or challenge their understanding of themselves.
- Can be caring towards each other.

22 – 36 months
- Learn social skills, and enjoy being with and talking to adults and other children.
- Seek out others to share experiences.
- Respond to the feelings and wishes of others.

You will find suggestions for *Look, listen and note*, *Effective practice* and *Planning and resourcing* in the EYFS Practice Guidance.

Personal, Social and Emotional Development

Personal, Social and Emotional Development
Making Relationships (Birth – 11 months)

Development matters	Play and practical support
Enjoy the company of others and are sociable from birth. Depend on close attachments with a special person within their setting.	Give young babies a favourite or preferred toy and encourage them to play independently under your watchful eye.

Sample activity	Shredded paper play.
Resources	A large bag of shredded paper from a recognised source to guarantee that it is clean and safe.
Health and safety	Ensure that the baby does not take too much paper into his mouth.
Layout	Prop the young baby in an inflated play ring so that he is comfortable. Place a few handfuls of the shredded paper into the play ring, across the young baby's lap.
The role of the key person	Sit and play with the shredded paper with the young baby for a few minutes, encouraging him to feel the paper crinkling in his fingers. After making sure that he is comfortable, sit to one side so that he can still see you, but let him explore the feeling of the paper by himself. If the young baby makes attempts to involve you in the activity, talk to him from where you are in a cheerful way, to help him feel safe to continue playing.
Note	The young baby might feel uncomfortable playing on his own, particularly if shredded paper is new to him. Try to start with an activity that you know he enjoys, and use your participation to make it fun.
Questions to ask/ suggested interactions	• Can you clap your hands in the paper?
Comments	Babies are more likely to explore new materials if you are there to reassure and encourage. If the young baby appears to be comfortable on his own, keep a watchful eye, but do not interfere. Respond when he makes gabbling noises or when he looks over to you, and join in with his play if he seeks to invite you.

Personal, Social and Emotional Development

Personal, Social and Emotional Development
Making Relationships (8 – 20 months)

Development matters	Play and practical support
Seek to gain attention in a variety of ways, drawing others into social interaction.	When communicating with babies, crouch down to their level to establish and maintain contact with eye, voice or light touch.

Sample activity	**Peek-a-boo.**
Resources	Nothing specific is necessary – just use what you have on hand.
Health and safety	There are no health and safety risks to this activity.
Layout	No particular layout is necessary, but it will work better if you are at a distance from the child.
The role of the key person	Sit watching the children in your group and seek to make eye contact with one of them. As they catch your eye, hide behind your hand, but peek around to see if they are still watching. Smile so that they know you are playing, but hide again, perhaps this time behind a toy or book. If the baby does not begin to move nearer to you, shuffle slightly nearer to them yourself. Keep changing the shield that you hide behind and moving nearer until the baby begins to move towards you. Keep playing until the baby is near enough to snatch up in a cuddle and a tickle.
Note	Note whether babies are able to be physically close and enjoy being with you.
Questions to ask/ suggested interactions	• Where's Helen gone? Here I am! • Try to make much of the game non-verbal.
Comments	Take care not to lose the baby's interest at the beginning by firmly reintroducing eye contact each time you come from behind your shield, smiling at the baby or babies playing. Try to play this right the way across the room to encourage a feeling of security that does not rely on proximity.

Personal, Social and Emotional Development

Personal, Social and Emotional Development
Making Relationships (16 – 26 months)

Code: PSED 3

Development matters	Play and practical support
Look to others for responses which confirm, contribute to, or challenge their understanding of themselves.	Use different voices to tell stories and get young children to join in wherever possible, sometimes using puppets, soft toys or real objects as props.

Sample activity	Puppet theatre.
Resources	A small selection of thematic puppets and a familiar story like *The Three Little Pigs*.
Health and safety	Ensure that puppets selected are appropriate to this age group.
Layout	Sit together at circle time, puppets laid out in front of you.
The role of the key person	When the children are seated, ask them if they know which story the puppets want to tell. Picking up the main character, tell the children that you are going to be the wolf and ask who would like to be the first little pig. Encourage the children to stay seated, but give out the puppets to the children around the group. Take the role of storyteller as well as the wolf and encourage the children with puppets to act out the story, while the other children join in on the repetitive chants such as 'I'll huff, and I'll puff...' etc.
Note	Note when, where, how and why you praise and appreciate young children and how they respond.
Questions to ask/ suggested interactions	• Who can remember what the pigs say when the wolf knocks on their doors? • And what does the wolf say he'll do next? • Do you think the pigs are scared?
Comments	Remember to include all of the children, even those who did not want to participate by holding the puppets. Remember to offer other children the chance to be a puppeteer next time; they may not want to volunteer themselves. Try to vary the stories but keep to a small, familiar selection.

Personal, Social and Emotional Development

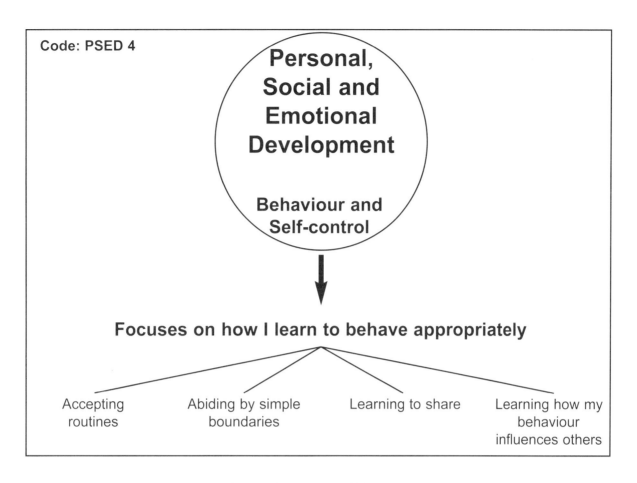

Code: PSED 4

Personal, Social and Emotional Development

Behaviour and Self-control

Focuses on how I learn to behave appropriately

Accepting routines

Abiding by simple boundaries

Learning to share

Learning how my behaviour influences others

Development Matters

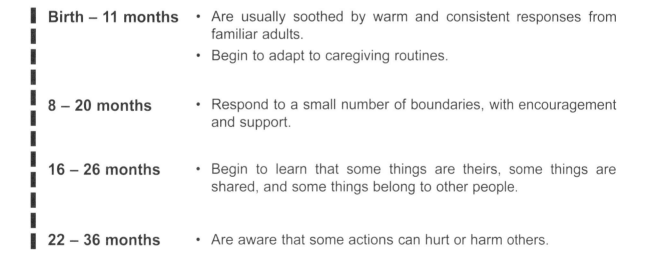

Birth – 11 months
- Are usually soothed by warm and consistent responses from familiar adults.
- Begin to adapt to caregiving routines.

8 – 20 months
- Respond to a small number of boundaries, with encouragement and support.

16 – 26 months
- Begin to learn that some things are theirs, some things are shared, and some things belong to other people.

22 – 36 months
- Are aware that some actions can hurt or harm others.

You will find suggestions for *Look, listen and note*, *Effective practice* and *Planning and resourcing* in the EYFS Practice Guidance.

Personal, Social and Emotional Development

Personal, Social and Emotional Development
Behaviour and Self-control (Birth – 11 months)

Development matters	Play and practical support
Are usually soothed by warm and consistent responses from familiar adults.	Provide experiences that involve using all of the senses, such as relaxing music, soft lighting and pleasant smells for the babies to enjoy.

Sample activity	A sensory session to relax and feel warm and secure.
Resources	If you have a sensory room you could select one calming light effect and calming music. A lamp projecting colourful images would be useful, but not necessary. Select a calming music-based CD rather than a sing-along tape. High on a shelf put out some calming lavender or peppermint oil.
Health and safety	Ensure that any scented oils are placed securely out of the babies' reach.
Layout	Lay out plenty of floor cushions and dim the lights to show your colourful images to their best. Use a coloured bulb in an ordinary lamp if you do not have access to any light effects. Play the music quietly so that you can still hear young babies vocalising.
The role of the key person	If possible select a time when you can give your attention to just one young baby. Lie next to them or sit facing them so that they can maintain eye contact with you. Talk soothingly to the baby, using baby massage techniques to make them aware of relaxing their arms, legs, hands etc. Talk gently through what you are doing and ensure that as much close eye contact is achieved as the young baby is comfortable with.
Note	Note when you provide opportunities for young babies to snuggle in. Is it only when you have time or is it in response to their needs? Try to avoid using it just at times when you are encouraging young babies to go to sleep.
Questions to ask/ suggested interactions	• Talk gently to the baby throughout this session. • Describe light and sound effects where relevant.
Comments	Before beginning this session try to discourage other staff from interrupting to borrow toys etc. Remember that many things arising in this session may also be included in other aspects of Personal, Social and Emotional Development. Talk to parents about significant events in the young baby's day. Ask them about important events at home and encourage them to contribute to their babies' records.

Personal, Social and Emotional Development

Personal, Social and Emotional Development
Behaviour and Self-control (22 – 36 months)

Code: PSED 4

Development matters	Play and practical support
Are aware that some actions can hurt or harm others.	Talk with parents about a consistent approach when responding to challenging behaviour such as scratching and biting.

Sample activity	Learning about 'No!'
Resources	A list of scenarios that you might discuss, particularly issues that have arisen in your group recently.
Health and safety	There are no health and safety risks to this activity.
Layout	Circle time.
The role of the key person	Sitting with your group talk about what 'no' means. Give an example that is common to your group, such as: 'Are we ready to go in yet?' while playing outside. Discuss what the 'no' response means in this situation. Change to another common situation, where a child might want a toy that you have. They ask for the toy and you say 'no'. What does this mean? So what might you feel like if they snatch the toy from you? Ask the children why the child may have taken it even though the answer was 'no'. Give the children options about what to do if this happens. Ask them if it is okay to hit out or bite or shout, or is it better to ask for help from an adult? Change the scenario and talk about another situation until you feel that the children are getting the message ... but be careful not to bore them!
Note	Note the way in which children respond to different people. Always listen to what they tell adults about their experiences.
Questions to ask/ suggested interactions	• Why do you think Anita might say 'no' if you want more dinner? • What can you do if somebody has taken your toy? • What do you do if somebody keeps saying no, you can't play with them?
Comments	Try to keep a list of occasions where 'no' has been used to little effect. Use this as an example in future sessions, possibly reinforcing this with a persona doll session.

Personal, Social and Emotional Development

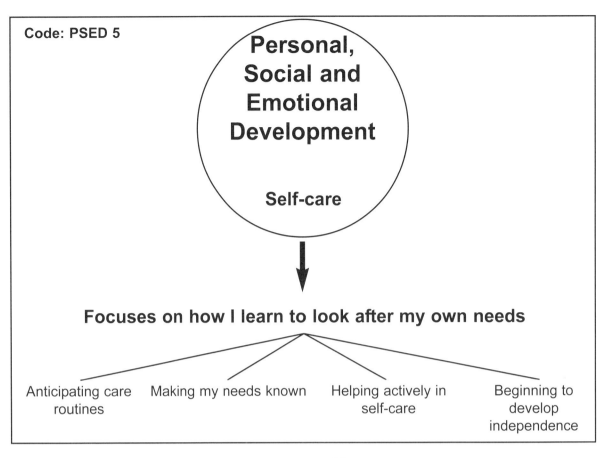

Code: PSED 5

Personal, Social and Emotional Development

Self-care

Focuses on how I learn to look after my own needs

Anticipating care routines

Making my needs known

Helping actively in self-care

Beginning to develop independence

Development Matters

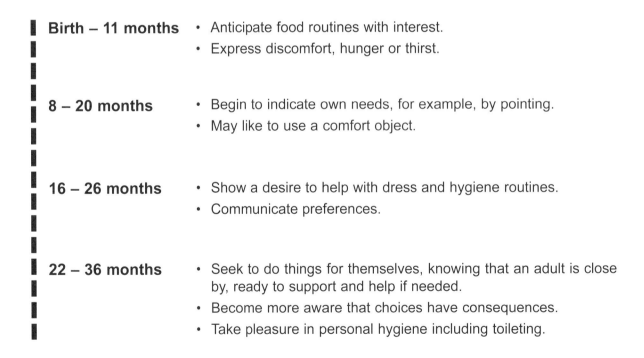

Birth – 11 months
- Anticipate food routines with interest.
- Express discomfort, hunger or thirst.

8 – 20 months
- Begin to indicate own needs, for example, by pointing.
- May like to use a comfort object.

16 – 26 months
- Show a desire to help with dress and hygiene routines.
- Communicate preferences.

22 – 36 months
- Seek to do things for themselves, knowing that an adult is close by, ready to support and help if needed.
- Become more aware that choices have consequences.
- Take pleasure in personal hygiene including toileting.

You will find suggestions for *Look, listen and note*, *Effective practice* and *Planning and resourcing* in the EYFS Practice Guidance.

Personal, Social and Emotional Development

34

Personal, Social and Emotional Development
Self-care (8 – 20 months)

Development matters	Play and practical support
Begin to indicate own needs, for example, by pointing.	Provide experiences that involve using all of the senses, such as relaxing music, soft lighting and pleasant smells for the babies to enjoy. Make the babies *want* to communicate by pointing.

Sample activity	Washing ourselves.
Resources	A low and secure water container that the babies can sit in safely. Bubble bath from a recognised children's range. Plenty of towels and face cloths. A relaxing CD to set the mood.
Health and safety	Ensure that supervision is appropriate to ensure that the water presents no risk of drowning and that the additional products used present no allergic threat to the baby.
Layout	Fill the container (to a safe level) with warm water, spreading some towels around the tub to soak up spills.
The role of the key person	Select two or three babies who get along with each other and dress them carefully in a suitable swimming nappy or similar. Get the support of another worker from the group. Sit the babies in the tub before adding the bubble bath and encourage them to feel relaxed. Gently scoop the water over the arms of the babies to ascertain that they feel comfortable with this type of play. Point out what is happening and encourage them to look at each other. Introduce the bubble bath by squirting some on your own hands, rubbing them together to show the babies the bubbles created. Smooth your hands over the legs of the babies, talking about the softness and the bubbles. Shake your hands in the water, making more bubbles. Talk to the babies throughout, encouraging them to splash gently and enjoy the experience.
Note	Note the ways you nurture babies' sense of themselves while also helping them feel they belong to the group.
Questions to ask/ suggested interactions	• Can you shake your hands and make more bubbles? • Arms up? • Are you ready to come out now?
Comments	Remember to keep the session short enough to ensure that the water does not get too cold.

Personal, Social and Emotional Development

Personal, Social and Emotional Development
Self-care (22 – 36 months)

Development matters	Play and practical support
Seek to do things for themselves, knowing that an adult is close by, ready to support if needed.	Talk to children about an activity and discuss with them what resources they need and where they might find them. Then encourage them to get things for themselves, so developing their sense of self-assurance.

Sample activity	Can I help you?
Resources	Coats and hats etc. for outdoors play. A group of co-operative and helpful children!
Health and safety	There are no health and safety risks to this activity, but care should be taken to ensure that help offered is carefully administered.
Layout	Take a small group of children to collect the coats and hats that they might need for playing outside and bring them into the room so that there is room enough to move about fairly freely.
The role of the key person	Pair children up with each other and ask if they can help each other get ready for playing outdoors. At the beginning show children how to hold their friend's coat so that it is easier to put on, but in later sessions try to leave them to it. Encourage the children to talk in their pairs about what is helpful, but also be trusting that their friends can help. Praise children who work well co-operatively together even if the end result needs input from you. Praise the children as a group for being clever and helpful to each other.
Note	Note how children express their own confidence and self-assurance by showing they value what they and others do.
Questions to ask/ suggested interactions	• Which arm do you think Alex should put in her coat first? • Can you hold the coat higher so that James can reach it easier?
Comments	Being helpful to somebody is a great way of gaining self-assurance, but be aware that younger or less able children might feel very frustrated if they cannot be helpful. Direct these pairs to help in different ways, such as helping to find the coat, or putting on a hat rather than a coat.

Personal, Social and Emotional Development

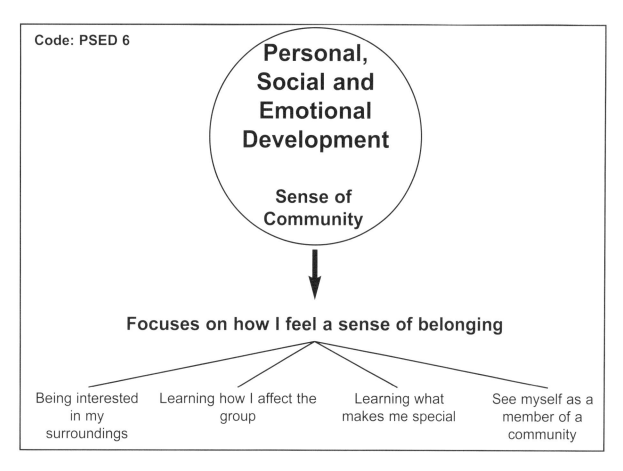

Code: PSED 6

Personal, Social and Emotional Development

Sense of Community

↓

Focuses on how I feel a sense of belonging

| Being interested in my surroundings | Learning how I affect the group | Learning what makes me special | See myself as a member of a community |

Development Matters

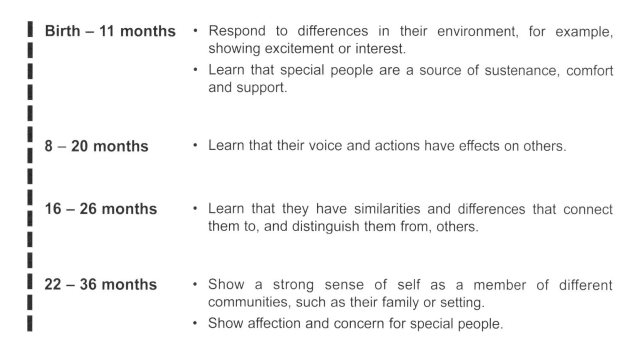

Birth – 11 months
- Respond to differences in their environment, for example, showing excitement or interest.
- Learn that special people are a source of sustenance, comfort and support.

8 – 20 months
- Learn that their voice and actions have effects on others.

16 – 26 months
- Learn that they have similarities and differences that connect them to, and distinguish them from, others.

22 – 36 months
- Show a strong sense of self as a member of different communities, such as their family or setting.
- Show affection and concern for special people.

You will find suggestions for *Look, listen and note*, *Effective practice* and *Planning and resourcing* in the EYFS Practice Guidance.

Personal, Social and Emotional Development

Personal, Social and Emotional Development
Sense of Community (16 – 26 months)

Development matters	Play and practical support
Learn that they have similarities and differences that connect them to, and distinguish them from, others.	Value young children's comfort objects and show them that you understand that they meet their emotional needs.

Sample activity	What's my favourite thing?
Resources	Ensure that each of the children present have their comforter with them if it is present in nursery on the day.
Health and safety	There are no health and safety risks to this activity.
Layout	Sit in a circle.
The role of the key person	Talk to all of the children about things that we all have, such as two feet, two hands, two eyes etc. and encourage them to point at the appropriate thing. Move on to things that we have in common but are different, such as different shoes on our feet, different coloured eyes etc. Then point out that we all have a favourite thing, taking care to point out that not all of us want to bring our favourite thing to nursery if this is case. Point out that these 'same but different' things are another thing we have in common and talk about the benefits of the favourite things from your group, e.g. Oliver loves his blanket because it's all warm and cosy, while Joel loves his silky because it reminds him of Mum and helps him not to miss her too much until she comes back.
Note	Note how, with your support and encouragement, young children begin to make decisions and develop preferences, thereby beginning to establish their autonomy.
Questions to ask/ suggested interactions	• Who has two hands? • Who has shoes on their feet? • Who has curly hair?
Comments	Don't forget to include dummies, teddies or other things that come to nursery intermittently, as well as identifying what your own favourite thing is.

Personal, Social and Emotional Development

Personal, Social and Emotional Development
Sense of Community (22 – 36 months)

Development matters	Play and practical support
Show strong sense of self as a member of different communities, such as their family or setting.	Provide a soft toy for children to take home in turn. It could have an overnight bag with a note to parents encouraging them, with their child, to care for it and return it safely.

Sample activity	Roll call.
Resources	Flash cards with each child's photograph and first name on it.
Health and safety	There are no health and safety risks to this activity.
Layout	Sit in a circle with your key group.
The role of the key person	Sitting the children together, start with the first name on the top and ask 'Who is this?' When the children respond, ask 'Is Max here?' If he is, welcome him to the session and encourage his friends to shake his hand or give him a hug. If he isn't in, ask the children if they can think what he might be doing instead, letting them know if he is having a day off with Gran, or is ill so that they can sympathise. Go through the whole group, welcoming everybody including other key persons.
Note	Observe the strategies children use to join in or avoid a group during play.
Questions to ask/ suggested interactions	• Max is not here, what do you think he might be doing? • Jim wasn't very well yesterday, do you think he will feel better soon? • Rachel had a day off yesterday. Can you tell us about your day?
Comments	Use this activity to develop a sense of belonging. Remember to ask children about their day if they weren't in, or if they feel better after being ill. Remember to prepare new cards for children joining the group immediately so that they can feel a part of the group straightaway.

Personal, Social and Emotional Development

Area of Learning: Personal, Social and Emotional Development		
Focus:	Age Range:	Code: PSED _____

Development matters	Play and practical support

Sample activity	
Resources	
Health and safety	
Layout	
The role of the key person	
Note	
Questions to ask/ suggested interactions	• •
Comments	

Ⓟ

Completed by: Date:

Personal, Social and Emotional Development
(0–36 months)

Date of activity:	Supervised by:
Children involved:	
Comments	

Date of activity:	Supervised by:
Children involved:	
Comments	

Date of activity:	Supervised by:
Children involved:	
Comments	

(P)

Communication, Language and Literacy

(0–36 months)

Communication, Language and Literacy
(0–36 months)

Section index

Selection of Sample Activities

	Birth – 11 months	8 – 20 months	16 – 26 months	22 – 36 months
CLL 1 Language for Communication	Page 45		Page 46 Page 47	Page 48
CLL 2 Language for Thinking		Page 50	Page 51	Page 52 Page 53
CLL 3 Linking Sounds and Letters	Page 55	Page 56		
CLL 4 Reading		Page 58		
CLL 5 Writing	Page 60			
CLL 6 Handwriting			Page 62	

A blank planner for you to copy and complete for the children is on page 63.

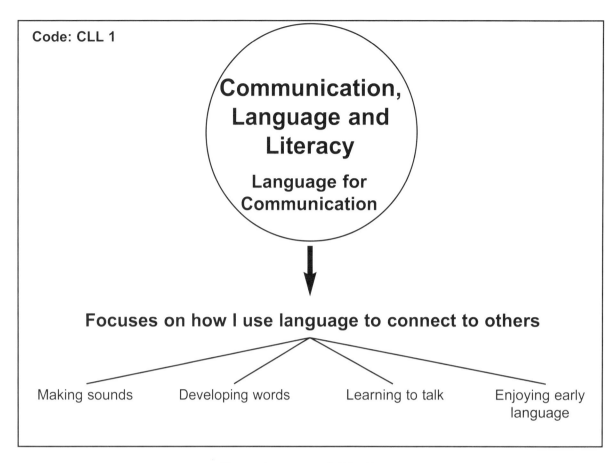

Code: CLL 1

Communication, Language and Literacy

Language for Communication

Focuses on how I use language to connect to others

Making sounds   Developing words   Learning to talk   Enjoying early language

Development Matters

Birth – 11 months
- Communicate in a variety of ways including crying, gurgling, babbling and squealing.
- Make sounds with their voices in social interaction.

8 – 20 months
- Take pleasure in making and listening to a wide variety of sounds.
- Create personal words as they begin to develop language.

16 – 26 months
- Use single-word and two-word utterances to convey simple and more complex messages.
- Understand simple sentences.

22 – 36 months
- Learn new words very rapidly and are able to use them in communicating about matters which interest them.

You will find suggestions for *Look, listen and note*, *Effective practice* and *Planning and resourcing* in the EYFS Practice Guidance.

Communication, Language and Literacy

Communication, Language and Literacy
Language for Communication (Birth – 11 months)   Code: CLL 1

Development matters	Play and practical support
Communicate in a variety of ways including crying, gurgling, babbling and squealing.	Use everyday routines such as dressing, changing and mealtimes to sing with, talk to and encourage babies to vocalise.

Sample activity	**Experimenting with our voice.**
Resources	Large pictures or models from our selected subject matter, e.g. farmyard animals.
Health and safety	There are no health and safety risks to this activity.
Layout	Sit comfortably facing your young baby or group of babies and ensure that the babies are comfortable with a clear view of your face.
The role of the key person	Choose a simple story with colourful supporting images such as *On the Farm* (published by Usborne) and read the story to your group. Using varying tones of voice, keep an interesting facial expression and eye contact with your group. Point out the farmyard animals in the picture and make the sounds associated with that animal. Encourage the young babies to join in, praising communication throughout. Remember to keep them fun and interesting, using the storybook as a loose outline for your story. Repeat phrases that have been well received and remember to include key phrases that the family might say for the baby to repeat also.
Note	Note the wide variety of sounds a young baby produces and how adults try to understand and respond to them.
Questions to ask/ suggested interactions	• What does the cow say? The cow says 'Mooooo'. • What did the farmer say? The farmer says 'Morning!' • Shall we read that story again?
Comments	It is never too early to introduce babies to story time. The key to success is choosing a small selection of stories, repeating them regularly and making them sound exciting but familiar. This went down extremely well, with the young babies who were still interested after the second reading. Shame I didn't have more time to read it through again.

Communication, Language and Literacy

Communication, Language and Literacy
Language for Communication (16 – 26 months)

Development matters	Play and practical support
Use single-word and two-word utterances to convey simple and more complex messages.	Provide everyday objects found in the home, e.g. a sponge, soft nail brush and plastic pan scrub for babies and children to explore, investigate and talk about.

Sample activity	What is it and what is it for?
Resources	Gather together a selection of items from home for a similar purpose, such as a sponge, face cloth, toothbrush and towel.
Health and safety	Ensure that items selected are new or freshly washed.
Layout	Sit together in a circle.
The role of the key person	Start this session by selecting the most familiar item and pass it around the group to handle. Ask the children: 'What is it?' When they have identified what it is, ask the children to say what it is for. Encourage miming of the use, but also a verbal description of it. Ask individual children: 'What is this for Shabanna?', occasionally encouraging them to tell you rather than show you. When they respond 'brush teeth' praise their input, and repeat it in a longer sentence: 'Yes, that's right, we brush our teeth to keep them clean.'
Note	Note the meanings young children generate in their language through the creative ways in which they combine words.
Questions to ask/ suggested interactions	• What is this? • What does it do? • How do we use it?
Comments	Use different collections of items to expand the children's use of words in very simple early sentences. Try kitchen items, clothing, writing implements etc.

Communication, Language and Literacy

Communication, Language and Literacy
Language for Communication (16 – 26 months)

Code: CLL 1

Development matters	Play and practical support
Understand simple sentences.	Spend time with young children sharing photographs, either in books or placed where they can be seen, e.g. on skirting boards or mobiles, showing family, friends, favourite foods or pets. Giving children a familiar context helps them to understand better.

Sample activity	'My family and other animals'.
Resources	Ask Mum or Dad to bring in a selection of photographs of family members, pets, favourite places etc. for each of your group. Ensure that they make notes on the back of each photo of who/where etc.
Health and safety	There are no health and safety risks to this activity.
Layout	Sitting with your group in a close circle but around the table.
The role of the key person	Select one child from your group each time that you schedule this activity and start the discussion by asking the particular child: 'Who is this?' and encourage him to tell the rest of the group about the people in the photograph. Use the notes from the photographs and your own knowledge of the family to prompt. Encourage others to tell the group about their own aunt or their own pet, or even their holiday in Florida, but remember that this session is about one child so return to this child and his photographs quite regularly. Finish the session with a group hug so that everybody feels valued.
Note	Note how adults and other children respond, e.g. mirroring, echoing, interpreting and sharing objects.
Questions to ask/ suggested interactions	• Does anybody else have an Aunty Jean? • Who can guess what Jack's pet fish is called? • Does it look like Jack is enjoying his holiday?
Comments	Try to pick the more demonstrative of your group to share this session first, encouraging them to share their photographs with others. Hopefully, when it is somebody else's turn they may be more likely to share.

Communication, Language and Literacy

Communication, Language and Literacy
Language for Communication (22 – 36 months)

Code: CLL 1

Development matters	Play and practical support
Learn new words very rapidly and are able to use them in talking about matters which interest them.	Use familiar photographs to introduce new words and encourage responses from children.

Sample activity	Who can leap like a little lamb?
Resources	None really required, but pictures of the animals you might be using may come in handy.
Health and safety	There are no health and safety risks to this activity.
Layout	A large, empty space with comfortable flooring.
The role of the key person	Start with some phrases that the children are familiar with and ask them to run like a rabbit or moo like a cow. Move in to new descriptives, demonstrating how to do it if the children look puzzled. Use phrases such as: Slither like a snake, leap like a lamb or pounce like a tiger.
Note	Note how children begin to use words in context, e.g. in questioning, imitating with understanding, playing, negotiating.
Questions to ask/ suggested interactions	• Who knows what a kangaroo does? • Kangaroos jump, but what else can we call that? • Can we remember the words we have learnt today?
Comments	Try to make yourself lists of groups of words to use in future sessions. Try different types of housing, transport, painting techniques etc.

Communication, Language and Literacy

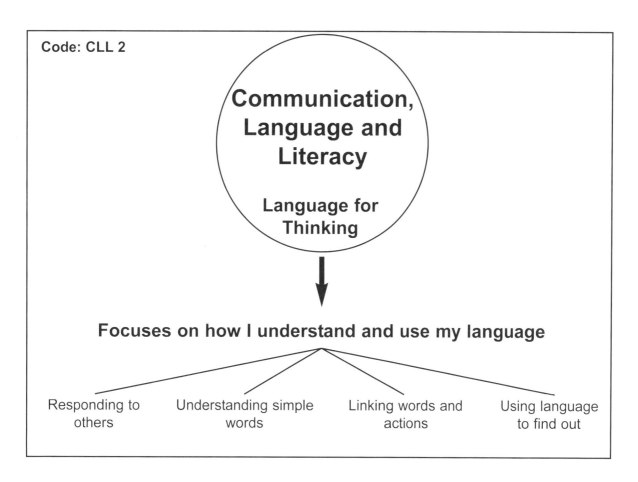

Code: CLL 2

Communication, Language and Literacy

Language for Thinking

Focuses on how I understand and use my language

Responding to others

Understanding simple words

Linking words and actions

Using language to find out

Development Matters

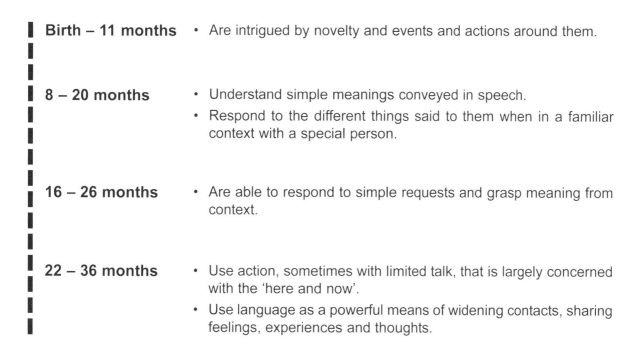

Birth – 11 months
- Are intrigued by novelty and events and actions around them.

8 – 20 months
- Understand simple meanings conveyed in speech.
- Respond to the different things said to them when in a familiar context with a special person.

16 – 26 months
- Are able to respond to simple requests and grasp meaning from context.

22 – 36 months
- Use action, sometimes with limited talk, that is largely concerned with the 'here and now'.
- Use language as a powerful means of widening contacts, sharing feelings, experiences and thoughts.

You will find suggestions for *Look, listen and note*, *Effective practice* and *Planning and resourcing* in the EYFS Practice Guidance.

Communication, Language and Literacy

Communication, Language and Literacy
Language for Thinking (8 – 20 months)

Development matters	Play and practical support
Respond to the different things said to them when in a familiar context with a special person.	Provide tapes of rhymes and stories, sounds and spoken words – some that require young babies to respond, others that encourage them to listen.

Sample activity	Listening to music and joining in.
Resources	A tape/CD with songs such as 'Old Macdonald had a farm' or 'Heads and shoulders, knees and toes'.
Health and safety	There are no health and safety risks to this activity.
Layout	Place the tape/CD player near to the key person so that popular songs can be repeated again and again to the children's satisfaction.
The role of the key person	Sit with a small group of babies and select a song to start the session that you know your group are familiar with, but do not sing along yourself. Getting the group's attention, encourage them to listen to the music, asking: 'What's that she's singing?', perhaps pointing to the speakers. If the children join in, use huge amounts of praise to encourage them to continue. If they do not appear to have made the connection, ask related questions such as: 'What does the cow say?' and wait for the moo sound to come from the tape/CD. Repeat the same song several times until the children are beginning to join in before moving on to the next song.
Note	Note the ways in which babies show you they have understood your request and note their responses to you.
Questions to ask/ suggested interactions	• Can you hear what the lady is singing? • What sound does the cow make? • Can we join in this time?
Comments	Try not to move too quickly with this activity, allowing the recognition of the children to dictate when to move on. Do not be surprised if younger babies in this group cannot make the connection without participation of the older children in this group. Mixed ability groups will benefit from the continuation of this activity, encouraging younger children to take to it a little sooner than they may otherwise do.

Communication, Language and Literacy

Communication, Language and Literacy
Language for Thinking (16 – 26 months)

Development matters	Play and practical support
Are able to respond to simple requests and grasp meaning from context.	Use puppets and other props to encourage listening and responding, e.g. when singing a familiar song, asking questions, joining in young children's play. Encourage repetition.

Sample activity	Simon says . . .
Resources	Whatever is at hand.
Health and safety	There are no health and safety risks to this activity.
Layout	Stand together in a circle.
The role of the key person	With this group of young children, keep your actions simple but clear. Start out by joining in with your action requests such as: 'Simon says put your hands on your head' or 'Simon says sit down on the floor.' When you are sure all of the children are listening and responding, stop doing the actions yourself and encourage the children to think for themselves. Towards the end of your session make your suggestions silly or fun, to reward the children's participation.
Note	Different kinds of activities encourage young children to listen and respond. Observe young children's reactions in play, to music, story, rhymes, TV and computer activities.
Questions to ask/ suggested interactions	• Simon says put your hands on your head and jump up and down. • Simon says sit down with your legs crossed. • Put on a silly hat.
Comments	At this early stage you should not expect the children to differentiate between the instruction preceded by: 'Simon says' and the one that isn't.

Communication, Language and Literacy

Communication, Language and Literacy
Language for Thinking (22 – 36 months)

Code: CLL 2

Development matters	Play and practical support
Use action, sometimes with limited talk, that is largely concerned with the 'here and now'.	Provide opportunities for all children to become part of a group, encouraging conversation.

Sample activity	Daily news session.
Resources	Nothing required, but paper and writing/drawing implements are an optional extra.
Health and safety	Ensure that writing implements are appropriate to this age group.
Layout	Select a comfortable area to sit and chat, providing sofas or cushions to make your group feel comfortable.
The role of the key person	Start the ball rolling by telling the group of something that you did recently that they might be interested in. Ask them if they might like to do that, or have done it before. Move on to a child in your group and ask what they did the day before or at the weekend. Encourage the rest of the group to listen carefully to what their friend is telling them. Try not to worry about taking turns if a child has news that relates to the conversation in hand, encouraging patience while listening to the news of others. Give all of the group an opportunity to tell their news, but don't press a child who cannot think of anything to say.
Note	Observe the ways in which young children make friends and note the attachments they make with adults and children, e.g. giving an object and taking it back.
Questions to ask/ suggested interactions	<ul><li>Hannah, were you about to tell us that you went to McDonald's at the weekend too?</li><li>Ava, did you forget that you went to visit your auntie in Wales?</li><li>Can we all listen to Leyleh's news and then we can chat about your news?</li></ul>
Comments	Take care to ensure that all of the children in your group do participate over a period of time, but it is not necessary that they do so every time. Talk with parents to find out news for a child who regularly finds it difficult to contribute and ask them about that specific item.

Communication, Language and Literacy

Communication, Language and Literacy
Language for Thinking (22 – 36 months)

Code: CLL 2

Development matters	Play and practical support
Use language as a powerful means of widening contacts, sharing feelings, experiences and thoughts.	Role play and dressing up, visits to parks, shops or libraries encourage children to take on roles, meet others, and express feelings and thoughts.

Sample activity	Role play: going to a restaurant.
Resources	Dressing up clothes to provide waiters/waitresses, chefs, customers on a posh night out etc. A dinner service/tea set/kitchen equipment and menu to choose from.
Health and safety	Ensure all role play implements are appropriate to this age group.
Layout	Set out the area for one or two tables of diners depending on the size of your group, a kitchen to cook in etc.
The role of the key person	Talk to the children about their experiences in restaurants and agree who will be staff and who will be customers. Encourage the children to select their favourite dishes to eat while the waiter writes down their selection and takes it into the kitchen for the chef to prepare. Talk about things we might do at a restaurant and encourage the children to chat about their own experiences or thoughts.
Note	Note what children say as they begin to combine words, ask questions, describe and predict.
Questions to ask/ suggested interactions	• Who has been to a restaurant with waiters and waitresses? • What did they do? • How is a table set at a restaurant?
Comments	Vary the role play to encourage different topics of conversation, but also to coincide with experiences of the children in your group – hospital, vets, hairdressers etc.

Communication, Language and Literacy

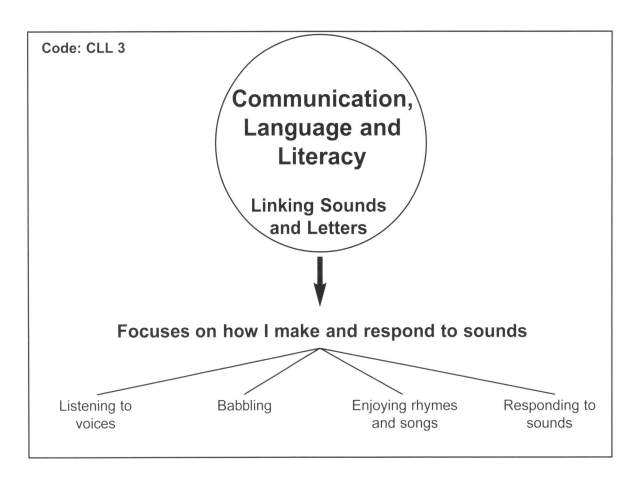

Code: CLL 3

Communication, Language and Literacy

Linking Sounds and Letters

Focuses on how I make and respond to sounds

Listening to voices

Babbling

Enjoying rhymes and songs

Responding to sounds

Development Matters

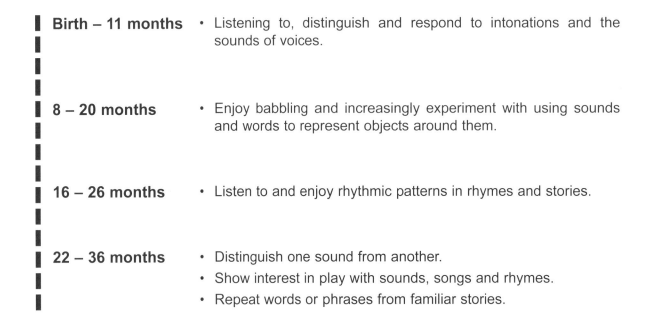

Birth – 11 months
- Listening to, distinguish and respond to intonations and the sounds of voices.

8 – 20 months
- Enjoy babbling and increasingly experiment with using sounds and words to represent objects around them.

16 – 26 months
- Listen to and enjoy rhythmic patterns in rhymes and stories.

22 – 36 months
- Distinguish one sound from another.
- Show interest in play with sounds, songs and rhymes.
- Repeat words or phrases from familiar stories.

You will find suggestions for *Look, listen and note*, *Effective practice* and *Planning and resourcing* in the EYFS Practice Guidance.

Communication, Language and Literacy

Communication, Language and Literacy
Linking Sounds and Letters (Birth – 11 months)

Development matters	Play and practical support
Listen to, distinguish and respond to intonations and the sounds of voices.	Have fun with babies by making a game of everyday activities, such as waiting for fingers to pop out of a sleeve, or head through a vest when dressing.

Sample activity	**Peek-a-boo after an afternoon nap.**
Resources	Gather together the clothes that you will dress the young baby in when they wake from their sleep.
Health and safety	There are no health and safety risks to this activity.
Layout	With the young baby ready to wake from her afternoon sleep make some space so that you can sit nearby and play comfortably with the clothes you will dress her in, and the sheets from her bed.
The role of the key person	Wait until the young baby is awake and ready to play. Start with the sheets from her bed and hide behind it. Peek from behind it and make eye contact while laughing. Then hide the baby's face with the sheet, asking 'Where's Holly gone?' When putting on clothes gradually, remember to point out hands hidden in sleeves, her head popping through her vest etc.
Note	Note the ways in which the gestures and sounds of very young babies change when you respond to them.
Questions to ask/ suggested interactions	• Where's Holly gone? • Where's Holly's hand gone?
Comments	This is often a time when caregivers can be rushing to prepare for the next session or finish their list of nappy changes. Remember that every opportunity helps encourage the child to become a skilful communicator.

Communication, Language and Literacy

Communication, Language and Literacy
Linking Sounds and Letters (8 – 20 months)

Development matters	Play and practical support
Enjoy babbling and increasingly experiment with using sounds and words to represent objects around them.	Encourage exploration and imitation of sound by providing objects such as firmly sealed yoghurt pots or plastic bottles filled with water, sand, gravel.

Sample activity	Making music from everyday objects.
Resources	Gather together a selection of things that make interesting sounds but are, of course, safe for this age group.
Health and safety	There are no health and safety risks to this activity.
Layout	Clear an area on the floor or on a table and lay out a selection of items in the centre, with space for the babies to sit around the outside in a comfortable circle or pop in and out as interest comes and goes.
The role of the key person	After selection of items, catch the attention of one of your group and ask them if they can make a particular sound. Watch as they try to imitate the sound that you have made with that object, offering support to shake their hand in the same way as your own, for example. As others join or interest is maintained, switch items and try to make different kinds of sounds. Use a balloon, a pan, an empty box as a drum, comparing the sound of each as you go along. Encourage the group to strike the instruments with their hands or a wooden spoon, even a dummy to explore different sounds.
Note	Listen to the sounds and early words babies use and how familiar adults show that they understand them.
Questions to ask/ suggested interactions	• Can Isabel shake this bottle like Jayne? • Can we bang this pan gently? • Now let's bang it as loud as we can.
Comments	Try to use different groups of instruments at different sessions, even sometimes using items that don't make sound but suggest them, such as farm animals, demonstrating that cows moo etc.

Communication, Language and Literacy

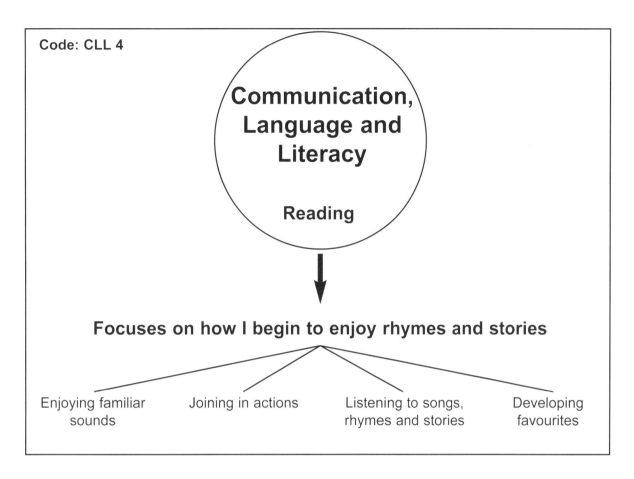

Code: CLL 4

Communication, Language and Literacy

Reading

Focuses on how I begin to enjoy rhymes and stories

Enjoying familiar sounds

Joining in actions

Listening to songs, rhymes and stories

Developing favourites

Development Matters

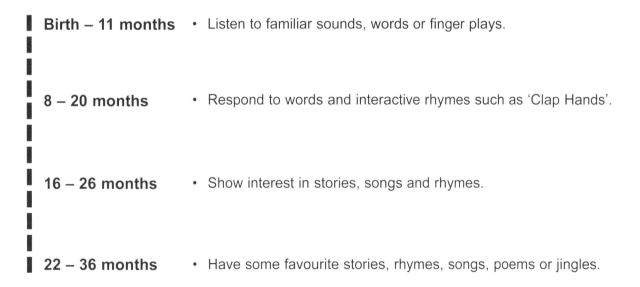

Birth – 11 months   • Listen to familiar sounds, words or finger plays.

8 – 20 months   • Respond to words and interactive rhymes such as 'Clap Hands'.

16 – 26 months   • Show interest in stories, songs and rhymes.

22 – 36 months   • Have some favourite stories, rhymes, songs, poems or jingles.

You will find suggestions for *Look, listen and note*, *Effective practice* and *Planning and resourcing* in the EYFS Practice Guidance.

Communication, Language and Literacy

Communication, Language and Literacy
Reading (8 – 20 months)

Development matters	Play and practical support
Respond to words and interactive rhymes such as 'Clap Hands'.	Collect and share stories and songs which parents and babies use at home.

Sample activity	Welcome to nursery.
Resources	Your knowledge of families in your group and the day book/diary etc.
Health and safety	There are no health and safety risks to this activity.
Layout	Nothing specific required, just a warm and welcoming environment.
The role of the key person	Make sure that you recognise and welcome each of the children into your room each session, paying special attention to the children from your key group. Make your welcome warm, using the parent's preferred name and the child's name, and ask: 'How are you both today?' or 'Did you have a good weekend?' etc. Take care to note down comments that may impact on the child's day, such as a disturbed night, a new tooth coming through etc. Let the baby *see* you reading and writing. Where applicable, take the child from the parent with a big hug, or welcome them with a hug if they have arrived on foot. Share a simple action song such as 'If you're happy and you know it, clap your hands'.
Note	Note verbal and non-verbal expressions of feeling which take place when babies are changed, fed, cuddled etc.
Questions to ask/ suggested interactions	• Did you sing your lovely song to Mummy last night? • Are you a tired boy already? • Ask Mum/Dad what they did to calm the child etc.
Comments	It is vital that as a key person you build up strong relationships with families from your key group, but not to the exclusion of others in the same environment. Remember that if a colleague is absent you will be sharing the care of their group temporarily, so it will be important that a relationship is established with all families to some extent. As you make regular use of the home-setting diary, make a point of sharing and celebrating what is in it with the baby, even if they are too young to understand.

Communication, Language and Literacy

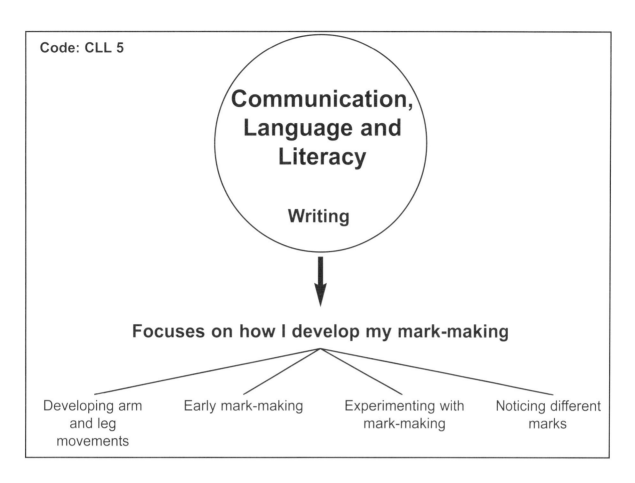

Code: CLL 5

Communication, Language and Literacy

Writing

Focuses on how I develop my mark-making

Developing arm and leg movements

Early mark-making

Experimenting with mark-making

Noticing different marks

Development Matters

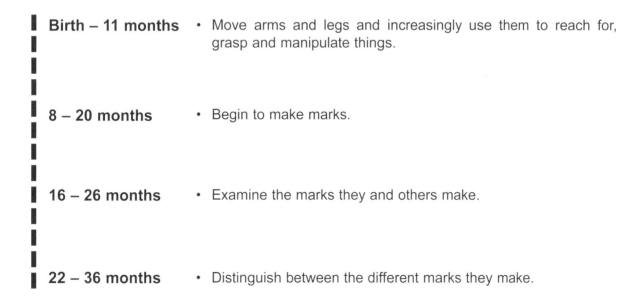

Birth – 11 months
- Move arms and legs and increasingly use them to reach for, grasp and manipulate things.

8 – 20 months
- Begin to make marks.

16 – 26 months
- Examine the marks they and others make.

22 – 36 months
- Distinguish between the different marks they make.

You will find suggestions for *Look, listen and note*, *Effective practice* and *Planning and resourcing* in the EYFS Practice Guidance.

Communication, Language and Literacy

Communication, Language and Literacy
Writing (Birth – 11 months)

Development matters	Play and practical support
Move arms and legs and increasingly use them to reach for, grasp and manipulate things.	Use gloop (corn flour and water) in small trays so babies can enjoy making marks in it.

Sample activity	Gloop.
Resources	Cornflour, water, food colouring, shallow trays or the trays from the young baby's high chair, an apron to protect the child's clothing.
Health and safety	Ensure that the babies involved have no allergic tendencies towards any of the foodstuffs to be used. Watch closely and wipe hands occasionally if the babies are putting hands to mouths regularly.
Layout	Sit the young baby comfortably in his high chair, carefully covering his clothes with an apron, covering any carpet underfoot with a washable surface. If the surface/tray to be used is white, add a very small amount of food colouring to the gloop on preparation.
The role of the key person	Sitting close to the young baby, place a small amount of the gloop into the tray and watch briefly for the young baby's reactions. If the young baby places his own fingers into the gloop and explores for himself, take a back seat and observe. If the young baby does not naturally explore the gloop himself, the key person could either take the baby's hands gently and place them into the gloop, making trails with his fingers as an introduction, or put his own fingers into the gloop to see if the baby imitates his actions.
Note	Observe babies and children as they make marks in food, water, spilt drinks etc. How do they respond to what they have done? Do they repeat the action?
Questions to ask/ suggested interactions	• Does that feel funny on your fingers? • Can you make a pattern on your tray?
Comments	If the young baby enjoys this activity, on the next occasion include a different colour gloop. As the baby gets older and more used to it, two different colours might be used, placed at either ends of the tray to encourage the baby to watch as the colours merge, or are mixed by his fingers.

Communication, Language and Literacy

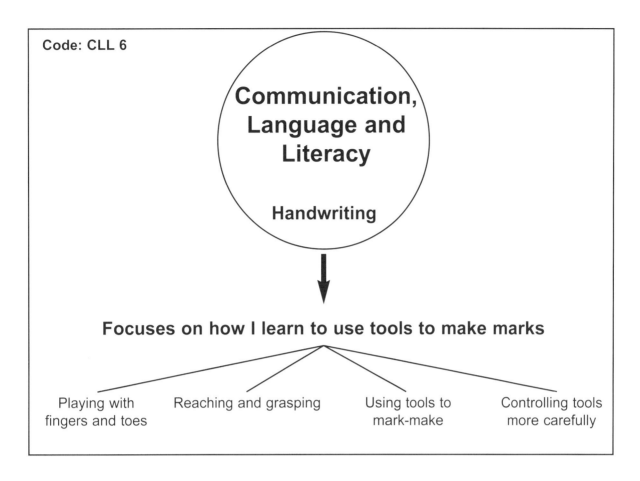

Code: CLL 6

Communication, Language and Literacy

Handwriting

Focuses on how I learn to use tools to make marks

| Playing with fingers and toes | Reaching and grasping | Using tools to mark-make | Controlling tools more carefully |

Development Matters

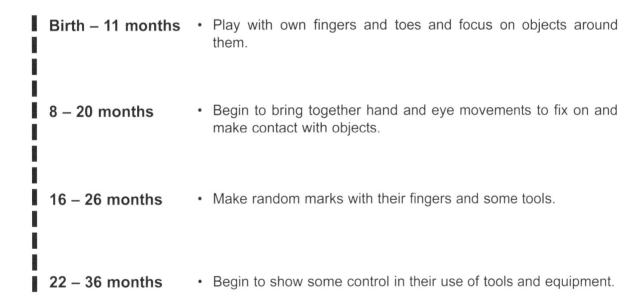

Birth – 11 months
- Play with own fingers and toes and focus on objects around them.

8 – 20 months
- Begin to bring together hand and eye movements to fix on and make contact with objects.

16 – 26 months
- Make random marks with their fingers and some tools.

22 – 36 months
- Begin to show some control in their use of tools and equipment.

You will find suggestions for *Look, listen and note*, *Effective practice* and *Planning and resourcing* in the EYFS Practice Guidance.

Communication, Language and Literacy

Communication, Language and Literacy
Handwriting (16 – 26 months)

Code: CLL 6

Development matters	Play and practical support
Make random marks with their fingers and some tools.	Discuss with young children what their marks represent and help them to understand that print carries meaning.

Sample activity	Free painting session outside.
Resources	A selection of paint pots containing very watery paint with big chunky brushes. Big aprons over warm coats.
Health and safety	The same care should be taken to ensure that the outdoor environment is safe as in usual outdoor play activities.
Layout	Clear a large space on a cemented area of the garden or use a large blank wall.
The role of the key person	Encourage each child in your group to select two or three pots of paint that they might like to paint with, and ask each of them to draw a picture of themselves playing on their favourite bike. Ensure that each child has a clearly identified section of the wall and try not to interrupt until each child stands back to appreciate their work. Without saying 'What's that?' encourage each child to tell you about their painting. Listen carefully so that you do not ask what 'this is' when the child may just have finished explaining in their own words. When possible allow the art work to dry before letting anybody else play outside so that the art work can be enjoyed by all. Remember that you may need to wash the paintings away before starting another session if there has been no rain.
Note	Observe early marks that young children make when given a crayon or brush.
Questions to ask/ suggested interactions	• Tell me about the red parts of your picture. • Would you like me to swap a colour with somebody else?
Comments	In hot weather this activity can be enjoyed without paint, just by using cold water. The children can change their drawings simply by letting the sun heat the surface and dry up the water.

Communication, Language and Literacy

Area of Learning: Communication, Language and Literacy		
Focus:	Age Range:	Code: CLL _____

Development matters	Play and practical support

Sample activity	
Resources	
Health and safety	
Layout	
The role of the key person	
Note	
Questions to ask/ suggested interactions	• •
Comments	

Ⓟ

Completed by: **Date:**

Communication, Language and Literacy
(0–36 months)

Date of activity:	Supervised by:

Children involved:

Comments

Date of activity:	Supervised by:

Children involved:

Comments

Date of activity:	Supervised by:

Children involved:

Comments

Ⓟ

Problem Solving, Reasoning and Numeracy

(0–36 months)

Problem Solving, Reasoning and Numeracy
(0–36 months)

Section index

Selection of Sample Activities

		Birth – 11 months	8 – 20 months	16 – 26 months	22 – 36 months
PSRN 1	Numbers as labels and for counting	Page 68			Page 69
PSRN 2	Calculating			Page 71	
PSRN 3	Shape, Space and Measures	Page 73	Page 74	Page 75	Page 76

A blank planner for you to copy and complete for the children is on page 77.

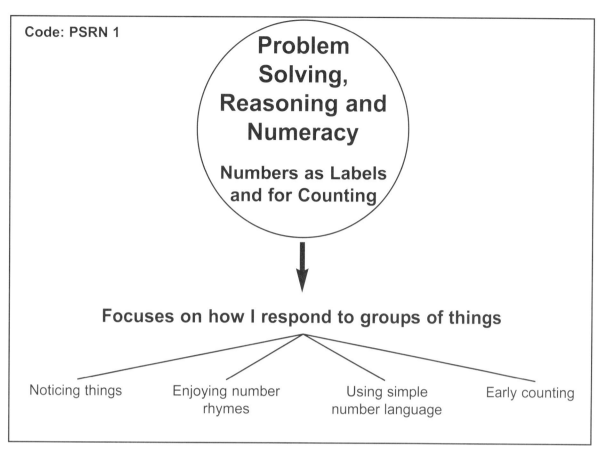

Code: PSRN 1

Problem Solving, Reasoning and Numeracy

Numbers as Labels and for Counting

Focuses on how I respond to groups of things

Noticing things · Enjoying number rhymes · Using simple number language · Early counting

Development Matters

Birth – 11 months
- Respond to people and objects in their environment.
- Notice changes in groupings of objects, images or sounds.

8 – 20 months
- Develop an awareness of number names through their enjoyment of action rhymes and songs that relate to their experience of numbers.
- Enjoy finding their nose, eyes or tummy as part of naming games.

16 – 26 months
- Say some counting words randomly.
- Distinguish between quantities, recognising that a group of objects is more than one.
- Gain awareness of one-to-one correspondence through categorising belongings, starting with 'mine' or 'Mummy's'.

22 – 36 months
- Have some understanding of 1 and 2, especially when the number is important for them.
- Create and experiment with symbols and marks.
- Use some number language, such as 'more' and 'a lot'.
- Recite some number names in sequence.

You will find suggestions for *Look, listen and note*, *Effective practice* and *Planning and resourcing* in the EYFS Practice Guidance.

Problem Solving, Reasoning and Numeracy

Problem Solving, Reasoning and Numeracy
Numbers as Labels and for Counting (Birth – 11 months)

Development matters	Play and practical support
Respond to people and objects in their environment.	Use feeding, changing and bathing time to play with young babies, e.g. finger play such as 'Round and round the garden'.

Sample activity	Exploring the garden on a bright day.
Resources	A comfortable reclining chair that can be placed in different locations in the garden. Warm outdoor clothes that are not too restricting.
Health and safety	Take great care to ensure that hands and faces cannot be scratched by shrubs, and that you do not choose shrubs with dangerous berries or flowers.
Layout	Choose an interesting part of the nursery garden that has low-growing plants or shrubs of different textures and different types of movement.
The role of the key person	Place the young baby (or group of babies) carefully among the plants so that the leaves blowing in the wind will blow across the young babies' laps and over their fingers. If you have a selection of different shaped leaved plants, move young babies to explore different textures, as well as feeling different shadows from the sun shining through the leaves. Ensure that scented flowers are included when available. Keep the session short in the colder months, but do not necessarily rule out this type of session if there is a light rain. Sensible dressing and short sessions are important considerations.
Note	Note how young babies use their senses to investigate your hair, jewellery, own clothes.
Questions to ask/ suggested interactions	• Can you hear the wind blowing through the trees? • Can you wriggle your fingers to make these leaves rustle?
Comments	If your own outdoor environment is not conducive to these activities, take a group of young babies for a walk in the park, parking the buggy for short periods near to different shrubs or flowers. In the summer young babies can be laid on a grassy area (after checking it for foreign bodies) to encourage them to feel the different textures of grass.

Problem Solving, Reasoning and Numeracy

Problem Solving, Reasoning and Numeracy
Numbers as Labels and for Counting (22 – 36 months)

Development matters	Play and practical support
Create and experiment with symbols and marks.	Focus on meaningful print such as the child's name, favourite cereal or book, or their age in order to discuss similarities and differences between symbols.

Sample activity	Sign lotto.
Resources	Gather together a selection of signs (including the numerals 1, 2 and 3) that are familiar to the children from their environment and copy them onto lotto cards. Choose stop and go signs, crossing patrol lollipops, no entry, familiar shop logos etc.
Health and safety	There are no health and safety risks to this activity.
Layout	Select a table for your session with enough chairs around the side for your group.
The role of the key person	Sit with your group around the table each with a lotto card. Start with the first symbol and ask: 'Matthew, can you tell me what this symbol means?' If Matthew can tell you, praise him and then ask who has this symbol on their card. If Matthew can't tell you, encourage the others to help him. Continue in this way until all of your symbols are gone, encouraging all of the children to tell you what they mean and help others.
Note	Note all the marks children make and how they 'tell' you what their 'products' mean.
Questions to ask/ suggested interactions	• Who can help Matthew remember what this symbol means? • Does anybody have a matching symbol on their card? • Who else is two?
Comments	An alternative way to play with these symbols is to have the children show you what the symbol means to them and encourage them to clap hands for the big '3' symbol etc.

Problem Solving, Reasoning and Numeracy

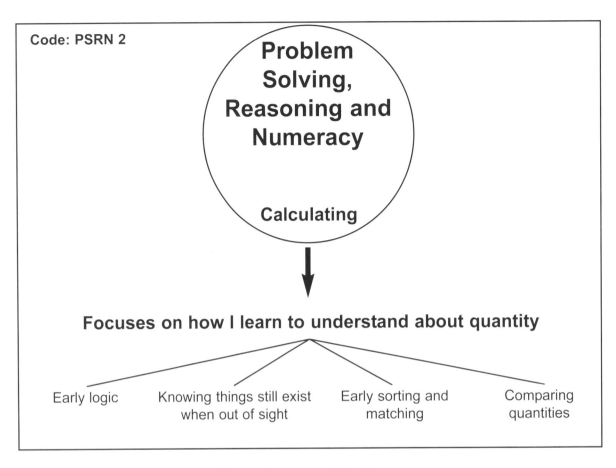

Code: PSRN 2

Problem Solving, Reasoning and Numeracy

Calculating

↓

Focuses on how I learn to understand about quantity

| Early logic | Knowing things still exist when out of sight | Early sorting and matching | Comparing quantities |

Development Matters

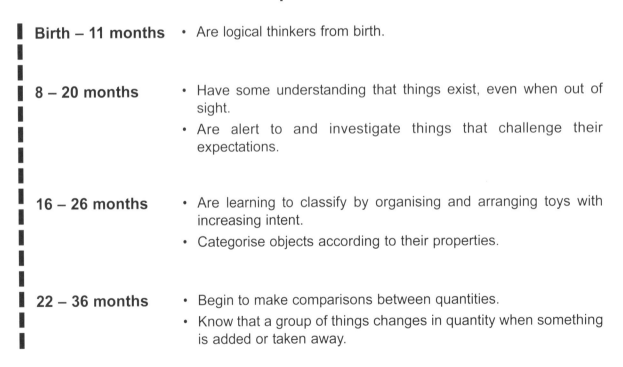

Birth – 11 months
- Are logical thinkers from birth.

8 – 20 months
- Have some understanding that things exist, even when out of sight.
- Are alert to and investigate things that challenge their expectations.

16 – 26 months
- Are learning to classify by organising and arranging toys with increasing intent.
- Categorise objects according to their properties.

22 – 36 months
- Begin to make comparisons between quantities.
- Know that a group of things changes in quantity when something is added or taken away.

You will find suggestions for *Look, listen and note*, *Effective practice* and *Planning and resourcing* in the EYFS Practice Guidance.

Problem Solving, Reasoning and Numeracy

Problem Solving, Reasoning and Numeracy
Calculating (16 – 26 months)

Development matters	Play and practical support
Are learning to classify by organising and arranging toys with increasing intent.	Even the youngest child can, with support, relish playing with sand (both damp and dry), water and playdough.

Sample activity	**A day at the beach in the sand tray.**
Resources	A selection of Duplo, Playmobil or other small world people and pets. A sand tray with half sand and a shallow end of water for the sea.
Health and safety	The same care should be taken as in any sand activity.
Layout	Before the children join the activity, set the sand out with families sunbathing, children making sandcastles and others in the water.
The role of the key person	Encourage the children to talk about what they can see and then take a step back while they perhaps relive a day of their own at the beach. While observing, try to throw in occasional pieces of food for thought, such as what might happen if the tide came in (you could add more water), or what might happen if the wind became strong (you could blow the water into the sand). Encourage the children to explore the thought of waves crashing onto the beach, or a dog splashing about in the water and into sandcastles.
Note	Observe how young children create new situations in their play, e.g. combining materials such as sand and water and transporting them from one area to another. Note how they sort and match into simple categories.
Questions to ask/ suggested interactions	• What might happen to that boy playing near to the edge if the tide comes in? • What might those people do to cool down if they get all hot? • Can you find all the animals?
Comments	Try different scenes such as dinosaurs in a prehistoric landscape or tractors on a building site. Introducing familiar equipment in an unfamiliar way will encourage children to see other things that might be added for extra enjoyment. Try not to say 'no' unless the piece will be destroyed by play in this manner.

Problem Solving, Reasoning and Numeracy

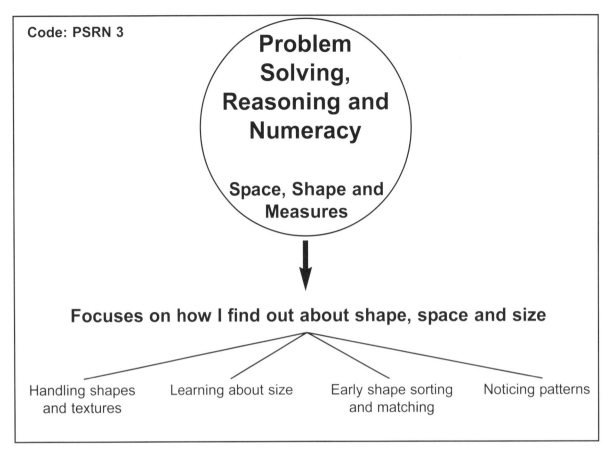

Code: PSRN 3

Problem Solving, Reasoning and Numeracy

Space, Shape and Measures

Focuses on how I find out about shape, space and size

Handling shapes and textures   Learning about size   Early shape sorting and matching   Noticing patterns

Development Matters

Birth – 11 months
- Develop an awareness of shape, form and texture as they encounter people and things in their environment.

8 – 20 months
- Find out what toys are like and can do through handling objects.
- Recognise big things and small things in meaningful contexts.

16 – 26 months
- Attempt, sometimes successfully, to fit shapes into spaces on inset boards or jigsaw puzzles.
- Use blocks to create their own simple structures and arrangements.
- Enjoy filling and emptying containers.

22 – 36 months
- Notice simple shapes and patterns in pictures.
- Begin to categorise objects according to properties such as shape or size.
- Are beginning to understand variations in size.

You will find suggestions for *Look, listen and note*, *Effective practice* and *Planning and resourcing* in the EYFS Practice Guidance.

Problem Solving, Reasoning and Numeracy

Problem Solving, Reasoning and Numeracy
Shape, Space and Measures (Birth – 11 months)

Development matters	Play and practical support
Develop an awareness of shape, form and texture as they encounter people and things in their environment.	Mobiles above changing areas, feathers to tickle and music to share, help young babies to enjoy being together and communicating with their key person.

Sample activity	Using the baby gym for a shared activity.
Resources	A safe and secure baby gym, interchangeable pennants to hang from it.
Health and safety	Ensure that the pennants selected are appropriate for your child's age group and that they cannot come detached from the gym causing harm to the baby.
Layout	Make the young baby comfortable underneath a baby gym with one or two pennants already selected for use.
The role of the key person	Sit close to one side and observe the young baby. Watch how she focuses on the pennants hanging from the gym, and then how she attempts to make contact with you. Responding to her communications positively should encourage more or different communications with you, taking the form of a conversation without words. Remember to maintain eye contact and change the pennants as the baby tires of them.
Note	Note the skills the young baby uses to make contact, e.g. inclining her head, wiggling her toes, making eye contact, banging hands/feet/objects, smiling and vocalising.
Questions to ask/ suggested interactions	• What can we see hanging here? • Can you feel the feathers tickling your hands and feet? • Do you like it when I do this?
Comments	Remember to vary the pennants hanging from the gym, the gym itself and, of course, the young baby's position; they could be lying flat for one session, half-raised the next time and propped quite upright for another. Plan each session to the changing skill level of the young baby involved.

Problem Solving, Reasoning and Numeracy

Problem Solving, Reasoning and Numeracy
Shape, Space and Measures (8 – 20 months)

Development matters	Play and practical support
Find out what toys are like and can do through handling objects.	Provide resources for babies to play with, e.g. pots and pans, wooden blocks, soft toys etc.

Sample activity	Role playing making tea.
Resources	A selection of pots, pans, cups, saucers, spoons and cooking equipment from the home corner. A representation of a cooker and sink is useful but not vital.
Health and safety	Make sure that water spilt does not present a risk of slipping.
Layout	Set out the table in your preferred format, perhaps using the tea set, with teapot for one session, the cooking materials for a different session.
The role of the key person	Sitting with your tea set, pour one of your group a cup of tea and ask them if they'd like one. Encourage the children in your group to pour a cup for you, or another in the group, matching cups to saucers etc. Remember to stir in the milk, sugar etc. talking throughout about what you are doing.
Note	Note how a baby follows any particular order – tea, sugar, milk etc. before stirring the cup.
Questions to ask/ suggested interactions	• Who would like a cup of tea? • Would you like milk in your tea? • Can we match this blue cup with a blue saucer?
Comments	Vary the activity when circumstances permit by using water in the teapot, possibly milk in the milk jug etc.

Problem Solving, Reasoning and Numeracy

Problem Solving, Reasoning and Numeracy
Shape, Space and Measures (16 – 26 months)

Development matters	Play and practical support
Use blocks to create their own simple structures and arrangements.	Have transparent boxes clearly labelled with a picture outline of the object, or the real object stuck on, so children can see where things belong and can return them safely.

Sample activity	Road safety in the garden.
Resources	A selection of bikes, prams etc. suitable for your age group. An improvised zebra crossing, traffic lights, lollipop and school crossing patrol outfit, police outfit. Large cardboard boxes.
Health and safety	Remove any staples on the boxes for safety.
Layout	Set out a roadway for the bikes, a path for pedestrians and prams with the selected outfits laid out adjacent to the appropriate equipment. Encourage the children to arrange the boxes to represent buildings.
The role of the key person	With your small group encourage the children to choose which role they will play – crossing patrol, police officer, pedestrian, motorist etc. Make sure that you select one yourself. Encourage the children to play freely, but always considering the rules of the road. Change traffic lights to red and encourage cars to stop while others cross. Pedestrians at the side of the road near to a zebra crossing suggest that cars might stop . . . but also might not. Talk the children through the activity, encouraging them to play safely.
Note	Note anything which tells you about a young child's concerns or preoccupations.
Questions to ask/ suggested interactions	• We have a red light. What does that mean? • Oh no! This car went through the red light. What should the police officer do? • Who lives here?
Comments	This might be difficult where outside space is not always easily available. However, the activity can still be enjoyed indoors with children wearing cardboard box tabards to represent cars etc.

Problem Solving, Reasoning and Numeracy

Problem Solving, Reasoning and Numeracy
Shape, Space and Measures (22 – 36 months)

Development matters	Play and practical support
Begin to categorise objects according to properties such as shape or size.	Thoroughly investigate environments with children, e.g. when outside consider how to shift leaves off a path, enlarge a puddle, or collect water from a dripping tap.

Sample activity	Matching and making sets.
Resources	Either a selection of different items that are half of a pair or part of a set or photographs to represent such items.
Health and safety	Sensible selection of items for inclusion should mean that there are no health and safety risks in this activity.
Layout	A table with chairs around. A pile of your gathered items in the middle.
The role of the key person	Introduce your session to the children by talking about things that are pairs or sets that the children are familiar with. Start with the most obvious and find one of two socks (for example) from the pile, asking the children if they can find the other. Move on to other simple pairs before changing slightly and going for a set like toothbrush and toothpaste, or umbrella and raincoat etc.
Note	Note those children who distinguish between big and small blocks, or know when tidying up, that different kinds of toys go in different containers.
Questions to ask/ suggested interactions	• What might we use this umbrella for? • So which of these things might we pair it with? • Can we pair this umbrella with anything else?
Comments	Remember that the children might see pairs or sets that you hadn't predicted, but these are not wrong. Using the examples above, the children might pair the wellies with the raincoat, but this, of course, is also correct.

Problem Solving, Reasoning and Numeracy

Area of Learning: Problem Solving, Reasoning and Numeracy	
Focus: **Age Range:** Code: PSRN _____	
Development matters	**Play and practical support**

Sample activity	
Resources	
Health and safety	
Layout	
The role of the key person	
Note	
Questions to ask/ suggested interactions	• •
Comments	

Ⓟ

Completed by: **Date:**

Problem Solving, Reasoning and Numeracy
(0–36 months)

Date of activity:	Supervised by:
Children involved:	
Comments	

Date of activity:	Supervised by:
Children involved:	
Comments	

Date of activity:	Supervised by:
Children involved:	
Comments	

Ⓟ

Knowledge and Understanding of the World

(0–36 months)

Knowledge and Understanding of the World
(0–36 months)

Section index

Selection of Sample Activities

	Birth – 11 months	8 – 20 months	16 – 26 months	22 – 36 months
KUW 1 Exploration and Investigation	Page 82		Page 83	Page 84
KUW 2 Designing and Making		Page 86		
KUW 3 ICT			Page 88	
KUW 4 Time	Page 90	Page 91		Page 92
KUW 5 Place			Page 94	
KUW 6 Communities		Page 96	Page 97	

A blank planner for you to copy and complete for the children is on page 98.

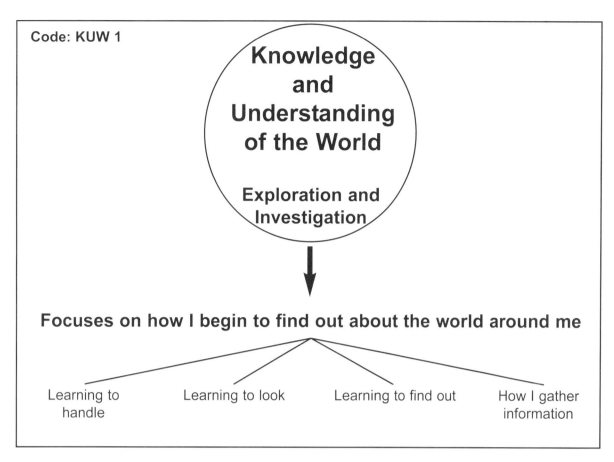

Code: KUW 1

Knowledge and Understanding of the World

Exploration and Investigation

Focuses on how I begin to find out about the world around me

| Learning to handle | Learning to look | Learning to find out | How I gather information |

Development Matters

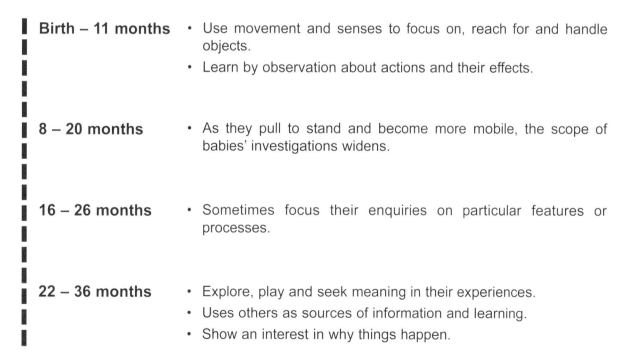

Birth – 11 months	• Use movement and senses to focus on, reach for and handle objects. • Learn by observation about actions and their effects.
8 – 20 months	• As they pull to stand and become more mobile, the scope of babies' investigations widens.
16 – 26 months	• Sometimes focus their enquiries on particular features or processes.
22 – 36 months	• Explore, play and seek meaning in their experiences. • Uses others as sources of information and learning. • Show an interest in why things happen.

You will find suggestions for *Look, listen and note*, *Effective practice* and *Planning and resourcing* in the EYFS Practice Guidance.

Knowledge and Understanding of the World

Knowledge and Understanding of the World
Exploration and Investigation (Birth – 11 months)

Development matters	Play and practical support
Learn by observation about actions and their effects.	Let young babies know you understand what they are saying, such as when they are hungry, tired, happy, sad and lonely. Use familiar routines to help them link cause and effect.

Sample activity	Lunchtime.
Resources	A comfortable chair, a bib, a bottle and/or lunch as required.
Health and safety	Ensure that all of the normal health and safety checks associated with lunchtime are in place.
Layout	If possible, sit yourself aside from distractions with the baby's meal requirements to hand.
The role of the key person	Talk to the young baby throughout the session, starting with the settling in period while the bottle is being warmed or food cooled. If the baby is restless and irritable, put words to their feelings: 'I know you're hungry, dinner won't be much longer.' Respond to the babies' communications throughout the session, whether they are verbal (crying or screaming) or physical (turning heads away or stiffening bodies). Whatever their mood, try to ensure a calm and soothing manner so that the young baby knows that you understand and that you are helping. If they turn their face away from the food, ask them: 'Have you had enough?' and perhaps offer a drink or next course.
Note	Note how young babies influence adult behaviour and the ways in which different adults respond.
Questions to ask/ suggested interactions	• Can you open your mouth for this little spoon? • Have you had enough? • Do you want something to drink?
Comments	Opportunities should be taken whenever possible to feed especially young babies with this approach. Of course, in a busy baby room it is not always possible. Similar opportunities may still be provided in a small group environment and this also adds different learning activities. Often young babies can be tired, hungry and uncomfortable all at the same time and we know that this often occurs just before a meal time. Try to time the babies' meal time to avoid this, but if this is not feasible use distractions and a calming manner to minimise their frustration.

Knowledge and Understanding of the World

Knowledge and Understanding of the World
Exploration and Investigation (16 – 26 months)

Development matters	Play and practical support
Sometimes focus their enquiries on particular features or processes.	Through play, young children can explore actions and emotions beyond their normal range.

Sample activity	Outdoor play with bikes.
Resources	A selection of bikes, cars and prams suitable for your group.
Health and safety	Ensure that bikes/cars/etc. selected for this activity are age-appropriate bearing in mind the abilities of participating children.
Layout	A big, open space to race up and down in.
The role of the key person	Take your small group outside and encourage them to race to the other end of the patio/play area. Resist the urge to follow them, encouraging any wanting your physical support to see how far they can get before you catch up. Encourage them to work out how to move quickly. If your group can manage the whole length of the play area without you, stay at the other end and encourage them to race back to you. If there are one or two who are anxious to go that far without you, turn it into a chase so that the group must ride their bikes or push their prams to catch up with you.
Note	Observe sounds and facial expressions as young children express feelings of frustration or anger as they separate from a carer.
Questions to ask/ suggested interactions	• Who can ride fast enough to catch me? • Can you push your pram right to the end to catch John?
Comments	Use different settings to encourage more timid children. Work with other key persons to swap groups intermittently to encourage children to be adventurous without your participation.

Knowledge and Understanding of the World
Exploration and Investigation (22 – 36 months)

Code: KUW 1

Development matters	Play and practical support
Explore, play and seek meaning in their experiences.	Provide non-specific play materials such as boxes and blankets so that play can move in different directions.

Sample activity	What happens if . . . ?
Resources	Nothing in particular is necessary.
Health and safety	There are no health and safety risks to this activity.
Layout	Circle time.
The role of the key person	Talk with your group about what it means to make choices. By this age they should be familiar with choices such as which table to play on, or who to sit by, but introducing the notion that choices might have consequences is often a difficult concept to grasp. Start with obvious questions, such as: 'What happens if we play out in the rain with no coat on?' and encourage the children to identify the consequences and why a particular choice might not be good/sensible etc. Include silly options, like what happens if I put ketchup on my cornflakes, and identify that although it won't taste very nice, it isn't really important. Move on to scenarios that require a little more common sense, such as: 'What happens if I jump up and down standing on my chair?' Hopefully the children will identify that they might fall off, they might hurt themselves or they might hurt others and agree that it would be sensible to choose not to do this.
Note	Watch the way children choose not to do things, as well as choose to do them. Note any patterns in what children consistently choose to do.
Questions to ask/ suggested interactions	• What happens if I eat the sand out of the sand tray? • Does it matter if I put my shoes on the wrong feet? • What happens if I don't come when somebody calls me?
Comments	Vary your scenarios according to the children joining in, trying wherever possible to use situations that could be feasible in nursery.

Knowledge and Understanding of the World

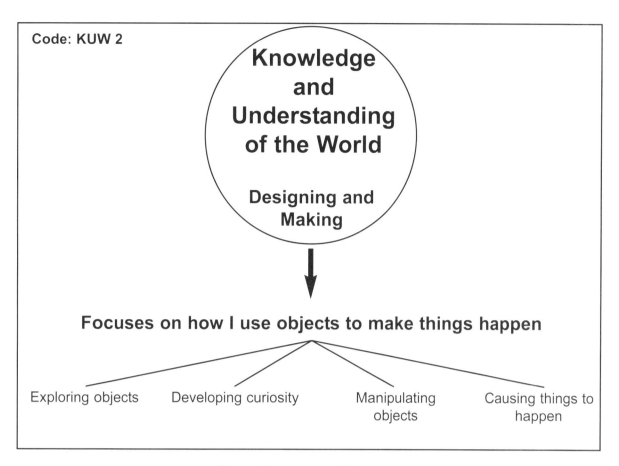

Code: KUW 2

Knowledge and Understanding of the World

Designing and Making

Focuses on how I use objects to make things happen

Exploring objects   Developing curiosity   Manipulating objects   Causing things to happen

Development Matters

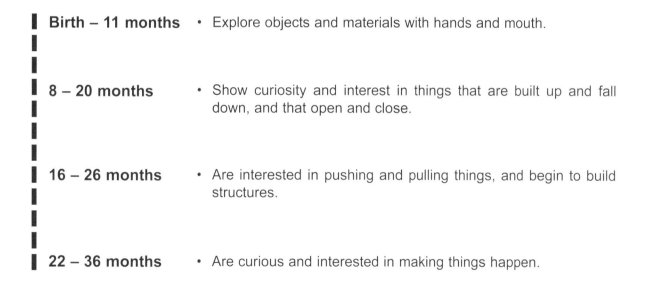

Birth – 11 months
- Explore objects and materials with hands and mouth.

8 – 20 months
- Show curiosity and interest in things that are built up and fall down, and that open and close.

16 – 26 months
- Are interested in pushing and pulling things, and begin to build structures.

22 – 36 months
- Are curious and interested in making things happen.

You will find suggestions for *Look, listen and note*, *Effective practice* and *Planning and resourcing* in the EYFS Practice Guidance.

Knowledge and Understanding of the World

Knowledge and Understanding of the World
Designing and Making (8 – 20 months)

Development matters	Play and practical support
Show curiosity and interest in things that are built up and fall down; and things that open and close.	Provide simple containers and lift-the-flap books which help babies and children focus on searching and finding.

Sample activity	Baby assault course challenge.
Resources	Gather together a selection of large play apparatus suitable for your age group, remembering to include items to walk around as well as climb over, crawl through and aim towards.
Health and safety	Ensure that challenges presented by the apparatus are commensurate with the babies' abilities.
Layout	Lay out a safe area on your carpet/matting with a clearly defined route from start to finish. Stack up safe cushions and use drapes and covers that can be drawn to one side.
The role of the key person	Guide each of your group of babies through the route in the manner best suited to their age/stage of development. Holding their hands or kneeling, go through the course backwards, so that they can come towards you throughout. Adapt the course for each child, but also with each pass, to take account of difficulties experienced or achievements made at the previous attempt. Provide encouragement throughout. Try encouraging other babies to sit and watch while they wait their turns, applauding at each successful pass.
Note	Note the ways in which babies indicate what they need, including help from the adults.
Questions to ask/ suggested interactions	• Can you duck down to go through this tunnel? • Now let's try to crawl over this little bridge . . . • Where is Gabriel hiding?
Comments	Remember to keep the assault course *very* basic, adjusting it for crawlers or walkers. Try to assist as little as possible, but remain aware so that where a baby holds out his hand to be held, you are there for him.

Knowledge and Understanding of the World

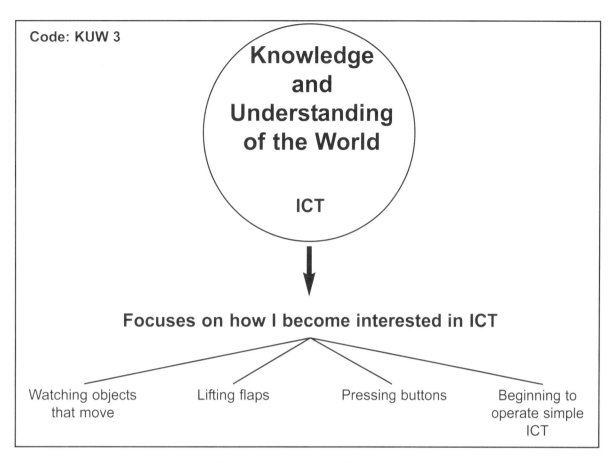

Code: KUW 3

Knowledge and Understanding of the World

ICT

Focuses on how I become interested in ICT

Watching objects that move | Lifting flaps | Pressing buttons | Beginning to operate simple ICT

Development Matters

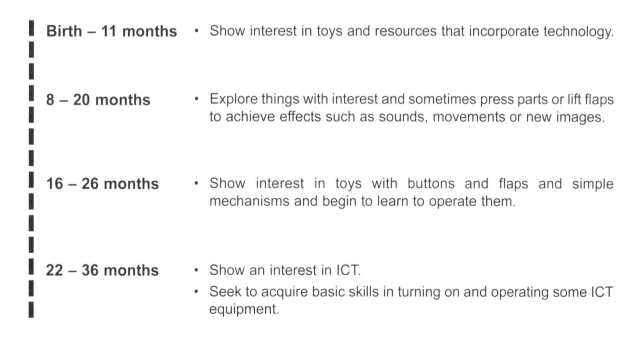

Birth – 11 months
- Show interest in toys and resources that incorporate technology.

8 – 20 months
- Explore things with interest and sometimes press parts or lift flaps to achieve effects such as sounds, movements or new images.

16 – 26 months
- Show interest in toys with buttons and flaps and simple mechanisms and begin to learn to operate them.

22 – 36 months
- Show an interest in ICT.
- Seek to acquire basic skills in turning on and operating some ICT equipment.

You will find suggestions for *Look, listen and note*, *Effective practice* and *Planning and resourcing* in the EYFS Practice Guidance.

Knowledge and Understanding of the World

Knowledge and Understanding of the World
ICT (16 – 26 months)

Code: KUW 3

Development matters	Play and practical support
Show interest in toys with buttons and flaps and simple mechanisms and begin to learn to operate them.	Make a diary of photographs with a young child to record an important occasion, e.g. finding a worm in the garden or visiting a special place.

Sample activity	What happens next?
Resources	A Polaroid or digital camera where possible, or a speedy developer nearby.
Health and safety	There are no health and safety risks to this activity.
Layout	The same layout and routine that happens on most normal days in your room.
The role of the key person	Talking through the day's activities is an important part of encouraging children to come to terms with their day in nursery and helps to form the skills required to predict. Use language that encourages the children to think about what they are doing now in relation to what happens next. Think about how you start your day. At one nursery the children all start together in one room, moving into the next at the same time every day. Take a photograph of the children moving from one room to the next and of what they will do when they get there (put the chairs around the tables ready for snack). Follow this throughout the day, taking photographs of what happens next on each occasion. Talk about how to take a photograph and show the children how to press the button when you hold the camera. Once developed, use this collection of photographs to talk about the day out of context, rather than what they really will do next.
Note	Note connections in young children's movements and activities, e.g. how they paint in circles, run in circles.
Questions to ask/ suggested interactions	• What do we do after snack time? • Then what happens? • What shall we photograph next?
Comments	Although they may be unfamiliar with the language used, you will find that children in this group have already developed a clear mind map of the routine of their day. Encourage them to choose what to photograph next.

Knowledge and Understanding of the World

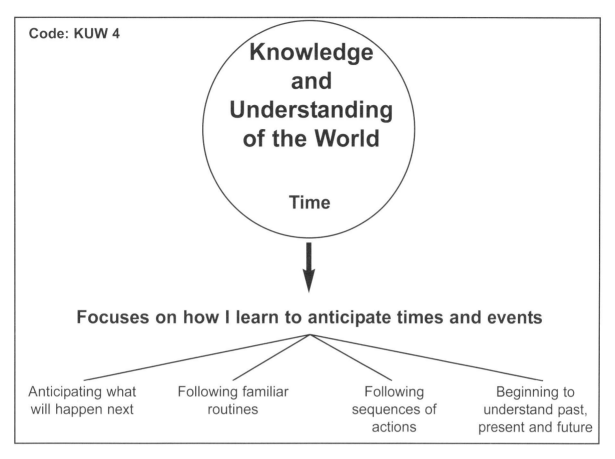

Code: KUW 4

Knowledge and Understanding of the World

Time

Focuses on how I learn to anticipate times and events

Anticipating what will happen next

Following familiar routines

Following sequences of actions

Beginning to understand past, present and future

Development Matters

Birth – 11 months
- Anticipate repeated sounds, sights and actions.

8 – 20 months
- Get to know and enjoy daily routines, such as getting-up time, mealtimes, nappy time, and bed time.

16 – 26 months
- Associate a sequence of actions with daily routines.
- Begin to understand that things might happen 'now'.

22 – 36 months
- Recognise some special times in their lives and the lives of others.
- Understand some talk about immediate past and future, for example, 'before', 'later' or 'soon'.
- Anticipate specific time-based events such as mealtimes or home time.

You will find suggestions for *Look, listen and note*, *Effective practice* and *Planning and resourcing* in the EYFS Practice Guidance.

Knowledge and Understanding of the World

Knowledge and Understanding of the World
Time (Birth – 11 months)

Development matters	Play and practical support
Anticipate repeated sounds, sights and actions.	Introduce baby massage sessions to reduce stress and make young babies feel nurtured and valued. Follow a set routine to provide reassurance and to encourage anticipation.

Sample activity	Getting to know each other.
Resources	The young baby's key person is all that is required. Calming music would be an added bonus.
Health and safety	There are no health and safety risks to this activity.
Layout	Make a space where the young baby can relax without too many distractions.
The role of the key person	This session is about building strong relationships with the young babies in your key group. Make the child comfortable but ensure that there is a physical contact – perhaps sitting in the crook of your arm, lying on your lap etc. Talk to the young baby about the things that you are doing and include baby massage techniques to ensure she is enjoying the contact. Ensure that all young babies in your group are offered the same individual contact. Follow a set sequence so that the babies can anticipate your actions.
Note	Observe and note the sounds and facial expressions young babies make in response to affectionate attention from their parent or key person. Note whether they begin to anticipate what will happen next.
Questions to ask/ suggested interactions	• Ask the baby if they are enjoying you stroking their arms.
Comments	This activity is extremely personal to each of the young babies in your group, and careful notes should be made about elements that the young baby has enjoyed, but most particularly those that they have *not* enjoyed. It is important that a strong relationship is developed between the young babies and their key person, but not to the exclusion of other workers in the group. Develop strategies among the team to deal with upset caused by staff absences.

Knowledge and Understanding of the World

Knowledge and Understanding of the World

Time (8 – 20 months)

Code : KUW 4

Development matters	Play and practical support
Get to know and enjoy daily routines, such as getting-up time, mealtimes, nappy time and bedtime.	Eating is usually a favourite activity! Talk to children about the choices they have made and encourage them to find new tastes to discover.

Sample activity	Taste testing.
Resources	A selection of fresh fruit and vegetables of different textures suitable for the children in your group.
Health and safety	Ensure that foods are not on the exclusion list for this age group and that pieces are appropriate and do not present a risk of choking.
Layout	Set your table out so that you and your group can sit around the table with room to lay out plates so your group cannot reach. Cover each plate so the children can only see the plates one at a time.
The role of the key person	Make your first selection something that the children are familiar with, and give them a piece to hold and taste. Observe their reactions, trying to put their expressions and reactions into words: 'You like that don't you?' or 'Was that not nice?' etc. Wait until each piece is eaten or discarded before introducing the next piece. Try to intersperse popular pieces with new tastes to encourage the babies to continue.
Note	Note how the environment (setting and adults) supports or might limit babies in expressing preferences and making choices.
Questions to ask/ suggested interactions	• Is that nice? • Does that feel crunchy? • Don't you like the tomato?
Comments	You could change this to be different types of food such as different bread – fresh, toasted, crusty, breadsticks etc. Don't forget to check that none of your group are wheat or gluten intolerant and that bread doesn't include nuts or seeds! Try to stick to five or six different tastes, repeating the exercise with the same fruit at intervals as baby's taste changes. Note down reactions to pass on to parents and other workers.

Knowledge and Understanding of the World
Time (22 – 36 months)

Code : KUW 4

Development matters	Play and practical support
Anticipate specific time-based events such as mealtimes or home time.	Use natural routines and situations to help children anticipate and learn.

Sample activity	Making a deal.
Resources	Whatever it is that the children are hoping to do as well as what you are planning to do.
Health and safety	There are no health and safety risks to this activity.
Layout	Your usual activity space.
The role of the key person	This is an opportunity to seize whenever the children are a little reluctant to do whatever you have planned. Sitting calmly in your group, explain to the children that it is not time for your group to play with the hamster (or whatever it is you are playing with). Tell them that if they help you tidy up really carefully you might be able to find time with the hamster when Group 2 have finished. For some children this will be immediately acceptable, but for others they may need regular reminders while tidying up to get the task finished.
Note	From what children do and say, note how they show what they understand, e.g. actions, questions, new words.
Questions to ask/ suggested interactions	• Do you think we can make a deal? • If I do that for you, will you do that for me? • If you let James play with that toy for five more minutes you can have it next. Is that okay?
Comments	Be careful not to promise anything that you cannot deliver. Also, take care not to make your bargaining points too far in the future so that the children are likely to forget about them. Try other simpler bargaining techniques in between, such as 'I'll draw you this picture when you have helped me sharpen these pencils.'

Knowledge and Understanding of the World

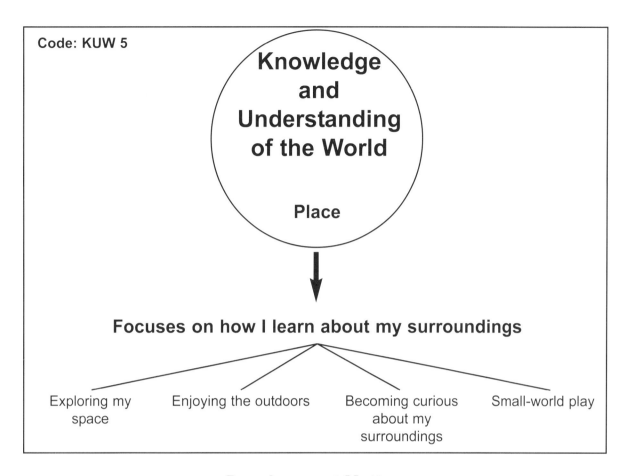

Code: KUW 5

Knowledge and Understanding of the World

Place

Focuses on how I learn about my surroundings

Exploring my space | Enjoying the outdoors | Becoming curious about my surroundings | Small-world play

Development Matters

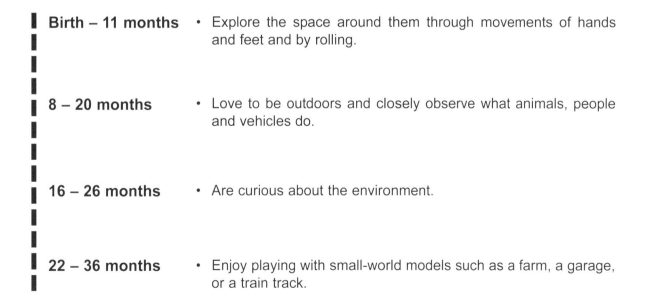

Birth – 11 months
- Explore the space around them through movements of hands and feet and by rolling.

8 – 20 months
- Love to be outdoors and closely observe what animals, people and vehicles do.

16 – 26 months
- Are curious about the environment.

22 – 36 months
- Enjoy playing with small-world models such as a farm, a garage, or a train track.

You will find suggestions for *Look, listen and note*, *Effective practice* and *Planning and resourcing* in the EYFS Practice Guidance.

Knowledge and Understanding of the World

Knowledge and Understanding of the World
Place (16 – 26 months)

Development matters	Play and practical support
Are curious about the environment.	Display and discuss photographs with young children that convey specific messages, e.g. a child in conflict with an adult, taking on a role, choosing a biscuit.

Sample activity	What shall we wear to go here?
Resources	A selection of enlarged photographs showing different climates or weather conditions. A selection of clothing to suit the photographs prepared, including sun hats, sunscreen, Wellington boots, gloves etc.
Health and safety	Ensure that sunscreen bottles are properly rinsed and the use of laces, ties etc. are properly supervised.
Layout	Try to lay the items out so that they are grouped together – gloves, summer hats, winter hats etc. Leave plenty of space for the children to move around in.
The role of the key person	Sit with the children in a circle and talk to them about the weather today and the clothes they have put on. Show the first photograph and ask the children to talk about what they see. Is it hot, cold, wet? After reaching a general consensus about the appropriate clothing, ask the children to select some things from the display to put on. Sit the children down again and discuss another photograph, encouraging the children to choose items that are appropriate. Make two or three changes of weather before leaving the children to play with the clothes unprompted for the rest of the session.
Note	Note the ways in which young children negotiate with adults and other children and the circumstances in which this takes place.
Questions to ask/ suggested interactions	• The sun is shining but there is snow on the ground – what should we choose to keep our feet dry and warm? • What kind of hat would we need to keep our ears warm in this wind?
Comments	Don't forget that you may need to help children put some things on or take others off. You will also need to provide a good selection of each item to fit the size of your group. Older children might take to this activity quickly, requiring less prompting before selecting the right clothing.

Knowledge and Understanding of the World

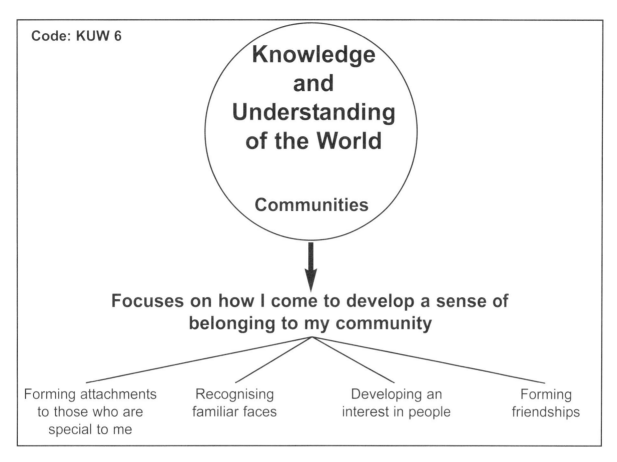

Code: KUW 6

Knowledge and Understanding of the World

Communities

Focuses on how I come to develop a sense of belonging to my community

Forming attachments to those who are special to me

Recognising familiar faces

Developing an interest in people

Forming friendships

Development Matters

Birth – 11 months
- Concentrate intently on faces and enjoy interaction.
- Form attachments to special people.

8 – 20 months
- Recognise special people, such as family, friends or their key person.
- Show interest in social life around them.

16 – 26 months
- Are curious about people and show interest in stories about themselves and their family.
- Enjoy stories about themselves, their families and other people.
- Like to play alongside other children.

22 – 36 months
- Are interested in others and their families.
- Have a sense of own immediate family and relations.
- Begin to have their own friends.

You will find suggestions for *Look, listen and note*, *Effective practice* and *Planning and resourcing* in the EYFS Practice Guidance.

Knowledge and Understanding of the World

Knowledge and Understanding of the World
Communities (8 – 20 months)

Development matters	Play and practical support
Show interest in social life around them.	Provide opportunities for babies to make choices, e.g. which spoon to choose, which bib to wear, the size of the paintbrush to use, to go outdoors or to stay in.

Sample activity	Making choices at snack time.
Resources	A snack that provides choice, such as white or brown, triangular or square sandwiches. A selection of bibs and cups/beakers to drink from.
Health and safety	Ensure that food, bibs, beakers etc. are commensurate with babies' ages and requirements.
Layout	Sit the babies around the table or in their high chairs in a semicircle in company with those around the table.
The role of the key person	Sitting talking with your group, place a selection of bibs in front of the children and encourage the children to select their own bib. Help the older children put on their bibs. Make this a really social occasion. Once ready to eat, hold a different sandwich in each hand and ask each child in turn which sandwich they would prefer, being quite specific about the choices available: 'Would you like a brown cheese sandwich or a white tuna one?', emphasising each sandwich as they are offered. Encourage older children to identify their preferences vocally, saying just 'white' or 'brown', while younger children can show their preferences by pointing or gesturing. Try to make options available whenever possible so that the children will understand (eventually) that sometimes there is choice, but sometimes there isn't.
Note	Try to understand and note the personal words babies create as they begin to develop language.
Questions to ask/ suggested interactions	• Would you like a square sandwich or a triangular one? • Do you want tuna or egg? • Shall I help you with that bib?
Comments	Offer babies choices that are commensurate with their age and stage of development, but do remember to talk about the choices available even with younger babies in this group.

Knowledge and Understanding of the World

Knowledge and Understanding of the World
Communities (16 – 26 months)

Development matters	Play and practical support
Are curious about people and show interest in stories about themselves and their family.	Create opportunities for young children to be involved in the domestic routines that link home and the out-of-home setting, being mindful of ways in which these may differ culturally.

Sample activity	**Nursery salon.**
Resources	A selection of hairdressing equipment such as brushes, combs, hairdryers and mirrors as well as hair colour charts, salon gowns etc.
Health and safety	Ensure that brushes etc. are regularly sterilised. Bottles should be washed thoroughly to remove all trace of the original product. Hairdryers should have the flex removed and mirrors be unbreakable.
Layout	Set out a few chairs for 'clients', mirrors for the 'stylists' to look into and a waiting area, but don't expect too much patience!
The role of the key person	Encourage the children to talk about who it is that helps them get their hair ready for nursery in the morning. Encourage them to talk about what Mum/Dad etc. does with their hair, role playing it on another child. Children whose hair needs nothing or little done to it before nursery should be encouraged to consider why. A shaved head clearly doesn't need brushing, but might need more trips to the hairdresser than somebody with long, curly hair. Compare hair colours to the charts and discuss the differences in the group.
Note	Note young children's questions about differences, e.g. skin colour, hair, friends.
Questions to ask/ suggested interactions	• Who helps you get ready for nursery in the morning? • What do they need to do to get your hair ready? • Do they do the same to their own hair?
Comments	Of course, your comments here will differ depending on the group, but you might need to make a note to gather together different resources next time. Clippers or oils might need to be improvised, or scarves gathered together to finish off the hair.

Knowledge and Understanding of the World

Area of Learning: Knowledge and Understanding of the World		
Focus:	**Age Range:**	**Code: KUW _____**

Development matters	Play and practical support

Sample activity	
Resources	
Health and safety	
Layout	
The role of the key person	
Note	
Questions to ask/ suggested interactions	• •
Comments	

Ⓟ

Completed by: **Date:**

Knowledge and Understanding of the World
(0–36 months)

Date of activity:	Supervised by:

Children involved:

Comments

Date of activity:	Supervised by:

Children involved:

Comments

Date of activity:	Supervised by:

Children involved:

Comments

Ⓟ

Physical Development

(0–36 months)

Physical Development
(0–36 months)

Section index

Selection of Sample Activities

	Birth – 11 months	8 – 20 months	16 – 26 months	22 – 36 months
PD 1 Movement and Space	Page 103	Page 104	Page 105	
PD 2 Health and Bodily Awareness	Page 107	Page 108	Page 109	Page 110 Page 111
PD 3 Using Equipment and Materials	Page 113	Page 114		

A blank planner for you to copy and complete for the children is on page 115.

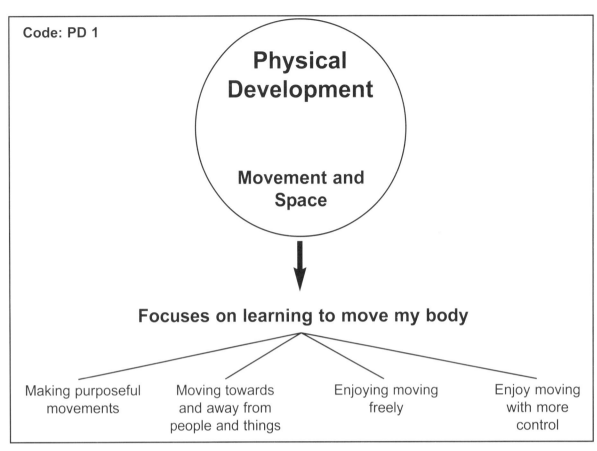

Code: PD 1

Physical Development

Movement and Space

↓

Focuses on learning to move my body

| Making purposeful movements | Moving towards and away from people and things | Enjoying moving freely | Enjoy moving with more control |

Development Matters

Birth – 11 months
- Make movements with arms and legs which gradually become more controlled.
- Use movement and sensory exploration to link up with their immediate environment.

8 – 20 months
- Make strong and purposeful movements, often moving from the position in which they are placed.
- Use their increasing mobility to connect with toys, objects and people.
- Show delight in the freedom and changing perspectives that standing or beginning to walk brings.

16 – 26 months
- Have a biological drive to use their bodies and develop their physical skills.
- Express themselves through action and sound.
- Are excited by their own increasing mobility and often set their own challenges.

22 – 36 months
- Gradually gain control of their whole bodies and are becoming aware of how to negotiate the space and objects around them.
- Move spontaneously within available space.
- Respond to rhythm, music and story by means of gesture and movement.
- Are able to stop.
- Manage body to create intended movements.
- Combine and repeat a range of movements.

Physical Development

You will find suggestions for *Look, listen and note*, *Effective practice* and *Planning and resourcing* in the EYFS Practice Guidance.

Physical Development
Movement and Space (Birth – 11 months)

Development matters	Play and practical support
Make movements with arms and legs which gradually become more controlled.	For young babies, provide different arrangements of toys and soft play materials to encourage crawling, hiding and peeping.

Sample activity	Let's make some music.
Resources	A selection of freestanding musical instruments safe for this age group. Include rain makers, bells hanging from a small carousel, maracas and as many different sounding and attractive instruments as possible.
Health and safety	Ensure that babies do not inadvertently bash themselves or others during this activity.
Layout	Arrange the instruments in a semicircle around the head of a floor cushion onto which you are to lay the young baby.
The role of the key person	Lay the young baby on her front with her head roughly central in the semicircle of instruments. Ensure that she can easily reach at least one of the collection and observe how she responds to it. Remember that there is no right or wrong way of making music with these instruments, but encourage her to bash, knock or shake the instruments to make interesting sounds. Watch as she moves her body, rolling to reach other instruments and rearrange the semicircle to ensure that she doesn't come to an empty space. Encourage her to use different methods of making sound, including banging loudly on the drum.
Note	Observe ways in which young babies show determination in going for what they want.
Questions to ask/ suggested interactions	• Can you shake your hands to make this maraca rattle? • Bash that drum as hard as you can.
Comments	Although this is a musical session, you can lay out the semicircle with any number of different toys. Try different teddies and soft toys with various textures, sounds and aspects. Remember not to overwhelm the young baby, and double check that she has not moved into the empty space deliberately before you fill it with something else.

Physical Development

Physical Development
Movement and Space (8 – 20 months)

Development matters	Play and practical support
Show delight in the freedom and changing perspectives that standing or beginning to walk brings.	'What is it?' is one of the earliest questions as a baby holds up an object, accompanied by a questioning facial expression. Provide interesting objects such as a squeaky toy.

Sample activity	Can you find . . . ?
Resources	Make use of the items generally scattered around a room.
Health and safety	Ensure that requests made of the babies are reasonable and possible for the babies to achieve, with no risk of furniture toppling as babies pull themselves up on things.
Layout	Make sure that there are a selection of items that the children in your group can reach by their chosen method of travel – shuffling, crawling, walking etc.
The role of the key person	Sitting on the floor, ask one of your group: 'Can you pass me that Elmo?', praising them when they do. As others become interested, ask for different things from around the room, pointing in the right direction if they look confused. Try also to remember things from different heights to give each of the babies involved a challenge for their next step.
Note	Listen to the sounds babies make and the words children use as they make friends, noting differences in the way they communicate with adults and other children.
Questions to ask/ suggested interactions	• Who can find the blue car? • Can Gabriel pass Andrew the big teddy? • Can Hope reach the tambourine?
Comments	Try to give each of the children involved something readily achievable, to foster the feeling of satisfaction. After this try to give each of the children a task that prompts them to try something a little more than they would normally achieve. Offer them support if they are trying to stand up against the table, or reach something challenging.

Physical Development

Physical Development
Movement and Space (16 – 26 months)

Development matters	Play and practical support
Have a biological drive to use their bodies and develop their physical skills.	Make opportunities for young children to feed themselves using fingers, forks and spoons.

Sample activity	**Going on a bear hunt.**
Resources	*We're going on a bear hunt* by M. Rosen & H. Oxenbury story book or CD.
Health and safety	There are no health and safety risks to this activity.
Layout	A big empty space and some obstacles to climb over, under or through.
The role of the key person	If possible try not to sit reading this book, but try rather to use it for reference or, better still, join in with the story told on a tape or CD. Encourage the children to walk through 'the mud', or climb up 'the mountain' or through 'the river' using appropriate ways of walking. Remember to take them slowly in the beginning, speeding them up to test your group on the return.
Note	Note how young children develop large motor skills for walking, climbing or jumping.
Questions to ask/ suggested interactions	• Can we pretend our feet are squelching in the mud? • Phew, this mountain is high! Are we nearly there yet?
Comments	Try this using *The little prince and the great dragon chase* by Peter Kavanagh, a different story in a similar vein, but lay out the room in advance to allow searching for Teddy etc. Vary the stories to incorporate the type of physical activity you are seeking to encourage.

Physical Development

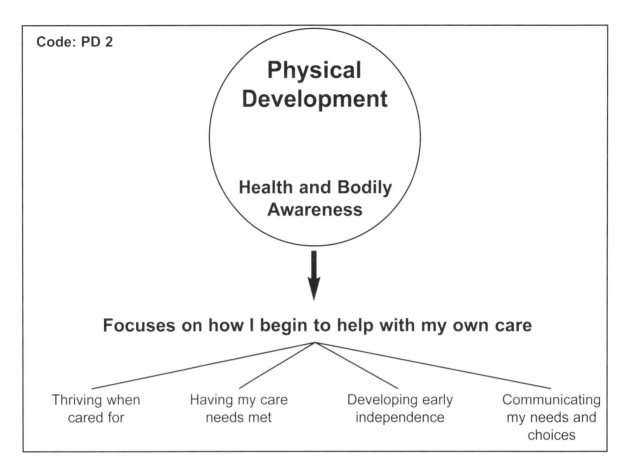

Development Matters

Birth – 11 months
- Thrive when their nutritional needs are met.
- Respond to and thrive on warm, sensitive physical contact and care.

8 – 20 months
- Need rest and sleep, as well as food.
- Focus on what they want as they begin to crawl, shuffle, walk or climb.

16 – 26 months
- Show some awareness of bladder and bowel urges.
- Develop their own likes and dislikes in food, drink and activity.
- Practise and develop what they can do.

22 – 36 months
- Communicate their needs for things such as food, drinks and when they are uncomfortable.
- Show emerging autonomy in self-care.

You will find suggestions for *Look, listen and note*, *Effective practice* and *Planning and resourcing* in the EYFS Practice Guidance.

Physical Development

Physical Development
Health and Bodily Awareness (Birth – 11 months)

Development matters	Play and practical support
Thrive when their nutritional needs are met. Respond to and thrive on warm, sensitive physical contact and care.	Encourage the young baby to gradually share control of the bottle. This provides opportunities for sensory learning and increased independence.

Sample activity	Afternoon snack time.
Resources	Something tasty for the young baby to eat suitable for his age and stage of weaning development, and a bottle to drink from.
Health and safety	Ensure that all normal snack time health and safety checks are undertaken, remembering to double check for babies who are still not used to much solid food.
Layout	Seated in a social group with his peers so that he can feel part of the group.
The role of the key person	Talking to the young babies in your group throughout this session is vital. Talk about the things that they are eating and how much they are enjoying it. Before the young baby is fully satisfied with his meal, put aside the bowl of food and exchange it with his bottle. Encourage the young baby to use one or two hands to help you hold his bottle, relinquishing your hold as the young baby becomes more experienced. Take care not to use this new found skill as a means of ignoring this particular young baby while you concentrate on others. Develop this skill as the baby moves on to finger foods to encourage a greater independence.
Note	Note young babies' hunger patterns and how they regulate the speed and intensity with which they suck.
Questions to ask/ suggested interactions	• Can you help me hold your bottle? • Clever boy! Can you hold it on your own?
Comments	It is easy to use a seated group time such as lunch or snack to chat with fellow workers, especially while young babies are busy eating. Remember that social chat among workers and children is an important part of our children's development, and young babies are no exception. Talk with your group of young babies about what they are eating, what will happen next or things that they can see around them.

Physical Development

Physical Development
Health and Bodily Awareness (8 – 20 months)

Development matters	Play and practical support
Need rest and sleep, as well as food.	Provide a comfortable and accessible place where babies can rest or sleep when they want to.

Sample activity	**Getting ready for a nap.**
Resources	A comfy place to sleep such as a dark and quiet room.
Health and safety	Ensure that all normal sleep checks are carried out.
Layout	Lay the room out with plenty of space for each of the tired babies, with floor cushions covered with a clean sheet and a warm blanket to wrap the baby in. Use calming music. Make sure you have the baby's preferred comforter(s).
The role of the key person	Adopt a calm and relaxing manner while preparing the room for nap time. Select a calming CD with the volume low. Prepare the baby for sleep in a calm, unhurried manner, trying to talk quietly and calmly without engaging the baby in chat. Gather together his comforters, blanket, dummy, teddy etc. and wrap him securely in a sheet. Lay him down, covering him with his blanket. Sit next to him, or nearby, perhaps stroking his cheek if that comforts him.
Note	Observe how babies' behaviour changes as they get tired and require sleep.
Questions to ask/ suggested interactions	• Try not to ask any questions at all during this period.
Comments	Observation of your key group should inform you of their preferred sleep time habits. Note them down carefully in case others may be caring for them at different times. If the child's usual pattern becomes disrupted, chat with parents or other carers to identify if a change has been identified at home or elsewhere and consider adapting your daytime routine accordingly.

Physical Development

Physical Development
Health and Bodily Awareness (16 – 26 months)

Development matters	Play and practical support
Practise and develop what they can do.	Support children in accepting choices made by other children and adults, even when this limits their own choices. Encourage them to practise and develop what they can do safely.

Sample activity	Safe opposites.
Resources	Make use of all of the things around you, but keep in mind unsafe issues that may have arisen in the past.
Health and safety	Care should be taken when discussing 'unsafe' opposites that they are not introducing a new and fun challenge for children to experiment with.
Layout	Sit in a circle.
The role of the key person	Talk carefully to the children so that they can sense the importance of the subject about keeping safe. Ask the group if they know of ways that they can keep safe, but with this age do not expect much input. Start with a recent example for impact. Ask the children if they would eat a piece of toast that has fallen on the floor. Respond dramatically if any say yes: 'Ugh! No! The toast will be full of germs from the floor. Put it in the bin and get a clean piece.' Use other examples such as sitting on a table or on a chair; keeping fingers out of the way of doors etc. Take opportunities as they arise to reinforce inappropriate actions by identifying *why* they are not safe.
Note	Note how you react when a young child makes a choice that you consider to be unhealthy, e.g. a child making a gun from building blocks, or children always bringing sweet things to eat at snack time.
Questions to ask/ suggested interactions	• What might happen if we sit on that table instead of a chair? • Why don't we eat Louise's sandwich that she started?
Comments	This is an activity that can be started off in a small group discussion, but is best returned to regularly to reinforce appropriate behaviour. As the children develop, the number of examples will increase according to their increased adventurousness.

Physical Development

Physical Development
Health and Bodily Awareness (22 – 36 months)

Code: PD 2

Development matters	Play and practical support
Communicate their needs for things such as food, drinks and when they are uncomfortable.	Provide stories, pictures and puppets, which allow children to experience and talk about feelings and needs.

Sample activity	**Going to the toilet.**
Resources	The nursery bathroom with appropriate toileting supplies.
Health and safety	All usual health and safety risk assessments related to toileting should be undertaken.
Layout	Nothing specific required.
The role of the key person	When a child has mastered the use of the toilet and is comfortable taking himself to the toilet, it can sometimes be a bit frustrating when clothing is not 'very helpful' and gets in the way. Accompany the child to the toilet as usual, but allow them to manage on their own as best they can. Watch closely for potential areas of frustration such as buckles or buttons, or if they come rushing in from playing outside and still have their coat on. Ask: 'Would you like me to help?' without assuming that the answer will be 'yes', and wait for a response before helping. Do only as much as is necessary to help the child continue, perhaps stopping when the troublesome button is undone. Praise the child for doing so much on their own and for remembering to ask for help in time.
Note	Note examples of healthy independence, e.g. a child playing happily with building blocks or looking through a window.
Questions to ask/ suggested interactions	• Would you like me to help you with that button? • Can you manage on your own? • Is that all you need me to do?
Comments	Make sure that your support does not undermine the child's ability and does not impinge on the child's self-esteem.

Physical Development

Physical Development
Health and Bodily Awareness (22 – 36 months)

Development matters	Play and practical support
Show emerging autonomy in self-care.	Offer choices for children in terms of potties, small toilets, trainer seats, steps, and recognise and support their fascination with bodily functions.

Sample activity	Getting ourselves dressed.
Resources	Hats, coats, wellies etc. belonging to each of the group.
Health and safety	There are no health and safety risks to this activity.
Layout	Collect coats etc. from the pegs and take them into a room with plenty of space.
The role of the key person	Try to encourage the children to do as much for themselves as possible without leaving them to it completely. Try showing them with your own coat that one arm goes in first while you reach around the back to put your other arm in the sleeve behind you. This is a difficult thing to get used to, so be patient. Once the coat is on, see if the children can do any or all of the fastenings on their coats, offering guidance to get children started or secure their fastening. Use exaggerated finger/hand movements to demonstrate, providing lots of support for those who don't want help.
Note	Look for ways in which children begin to develop fine motor skills, e.g. the way they use their fingers in trying to do up buttons on a coat, pull up a zip, pour a drink or use a watering can.
Questions to ask/ suggested interactions	• Can you reach your arm down and backwards to reach that sleeve? • Shall I hold the coat still so that you can find the opening to that sleeve? • Shall I do the first button and you can try the second?
Comments	How much support a child needs or wants may vary considerably from day to day depending on the coat and the clothes they are wearing. Support attempts to fasten buttons even if they are done up in the wrong order, not necessarily redoing them in the right way . . . after all, does it matter that they are done up incorrectly? Probably not. Praise the child for managing their buttons so well.

Physical Development

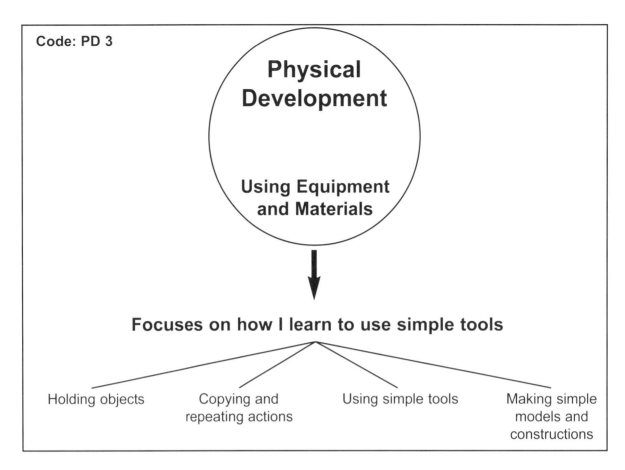

Code: PD 3

Physical Development

Using Equipment and Materials

Focuses on how I learn to use simple tools

Holding objects

Copying and repeating actions

Using simple tools

Making simple models and constructions

Development Matters

Birth – 11 months	• Watch and explore hands and feet.
	• Reach out for, touch and begin to hold objects.
8 – 20 months	• Imitate and improvise actions they have observed, such as clapping and waving.
	• Become absorbed in putting objects in and out of containers.
	• Enjoy the sensory experience of making marks in damp sand, paste or paint. This is particularly important for babies who have a visual impairment.
16 – 26 months	• Use tools and materials for particular purposes.
	• Begin to make, and manipulate, objects and tools.
	• Put together a sequence of actions.
22 – 36 months	• Balance blocks to create simple structures.
	• Show increasing control in holding and using hammers, books, beaters and mark-making tools.

You will find suggestions for *Look, listen and note*, *Effective practice* and *Planning and resourcing* in the EYFS Practice Guidance.

Physical Development

Physical Development
Using Equipment and Materials (Birth – 11 months)

Development matters	Play and practical support
Reach out for, touch and begin to hold objects.	Allow time to observe what babies and children do when presented with several options.

Sample activity	Take your pick . . .
Resources	A shelf or cupboard full of suitable toys.
Health and safety	Ensure that you are not offering babies toys that are not suitable for their age group.
Layout	Prepare a safe area for the young baby to play in after they have selected a toy.
The role of the key person	Carry the young baby over to where you store a selection of toys that you know he is familiar with. Hold him in front of the selection and ask him to choose which toy he would like. At first this might prove impossible as making choices can be hard for all of us. After a while he will get used to this as an option and make it easier. Until he is familiar with it you could try several methods of encouraging selection. Try pointing and asking: 'Would you like to play with Elmo?' and watching to see how he responds. Often you will be in no doubt if the toy is a firm favourite, but if in doubt ask again: 'How about the laughing cow?' and again watch for reactions. Carry on until a toy is selected and place the young baby safely to play with his choice. Introduce this form of choice gradually – making sure that it is not too overwhelming a selection.
Note	Observe the strategies young babies use to demonstrate their likes and dislikes.
Questions to ask/ suggested interactions	• Would you like to play with this toy car? • Can you choose one of these toys to play with?
Comments	Make notes about his selections, but also about the toys he has declined. Try offering these toys amid a different selection where they may become the first choice. Remember that the young baby is not likely to want to play with his one choice for very long, so prepare a selection of toys similar to his selection.

Physical Development

Physical Development
Using Equipment and Materials (8 – 20 months)

Development matters	Play and practical support
Enjoy the sensory experience of making marks in damp sand, paste or paint.	Discover from parents the imitative games their babies enjoy and use them as the basis of your play.

Sample activity	A very messy painting session.
Resources	A large empty tub such as a flat sand or water tray. Thick paint or coloured gloop. Large pieces of paper such as the reverse side of wallpaper. A table/work surface at the same height as the empty tub.
Health and safety	Make sure that products used do not present allergy risks to the babies involved. Babies will need to be supported to ensure that slippery paint/gloop etc. does not make them fall over.
Layout	Lay the table at the side of the tub to make an L shape. Put your paint/gloop into the tub and tape the paper onto the table. Lots of protective clothing for everybody participating, or babies stripped to just nappies.
The role of the key person	The most important thing in this session is to be as flexible as possible! Encourage the baby participating to explore the paint in any way she feels comfortable, but show her that painting on the lovely big piece of paper is a part of the activity, not something she might get into trouble doing. Encourage her to make patterns with her hands, whole arms, and even her torso or whole body if she chooses to climb in! Whichever method she prefers to explore the paint, try to offer the same method of making her mark on the paper. This may mean asking a colleague to remove the table, but tape the paper directly onto the floor so that she can sit or lie on it. Try not to direct her play too much, limiting your input to suggesting different methods to try.
Note	Note the differences between babies' imitations and the bodily movements which they use to recreate a situation, e.g. bouncing on the adult's knee.
Questions to ask/ suggested interactions	• How does that feel on your fingers? • Why not try your whole arms? • Can we make patterns with those arms on this paper?
Comments	This is not an activity for the faint-hearted! Try this when your numbers are low, or when you have the extra support of volunteers or helpers to avoid ending up with paint all over everybody else's clothing.

Physical Development

Area of Learning: Physical Development		
Focus:	**Age Range:**	**Code: PD** _____

Development matters	Play and practical support

Sample activity	
Resources	
Health and safety	
Layout	
The role of the key person	
Note	
Questions to ask/ suggested interactions	• •
Comments	

Ⓟ

Completed by: **Date:**

Physical Development
(0–36 months)

Date of activity:	Supervised by:
Children involved:	
Comments	

Date of activity:	Supervised by:
Children involved:	
Comments	

Date of activity:	Supervised by:
Children involved:	
Comments	

(P)

Creative Development

(0–36 months)

Creative Development
(0–36 months)

Section index

Selection of Sample Activities

A blank planner for you to copy and complete for the children is on page 131.

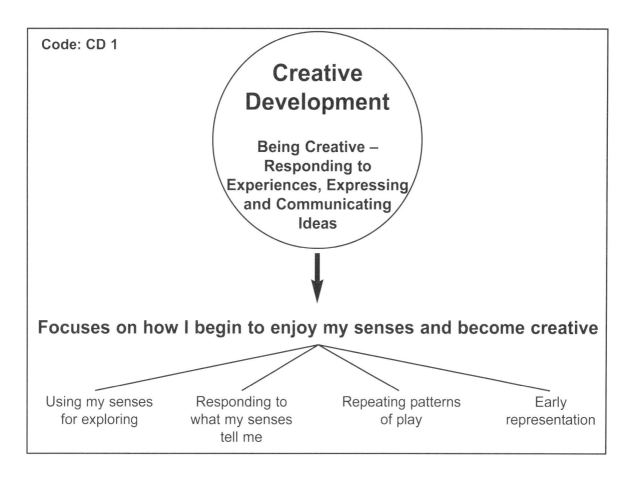

Code: CD 1

Creative Development

Being Creative – Responding to Experiences, Expressing and Communicating Ideas

Focuses on how I begin to enjoy my senses and become creative

| Using my senses for exploring | Responding to what my senses tell me | Repeating patterns of play | Early representation |

Development Matters

Birth – 11 months
- Use movement and sensory exploration to connect with their immediate environment.

8 – 20 months
- Respond to what they see, hear, smell, touch and feel.

16 – 26 months
- Express themselves through physical action and sound.
- Explore by repeating patterns of play.

22 – 36 months
- Seek to make sense of what they see, hear, smell, touch and feel.
- Begin to use representation as a form of communication.

You will find suggestions for *Look, listen and note*, *Effective practice* and *Planning and resourcing* in the EYFS Practice Guidance.

Creative Development

Creative Development
Being Creative – Responding to Experiences ... (Birth – 11 months) Code: CD 1

Development matters	Play and practical support
Use movement and sensory exploration to connect with their immediate environment.	Use finger play, rhymes and familiar songs from home to support young babies exploration and enjoyment in learning about their bodies and environment.

Sample activity	'This little piggy . . .'
Resources	None required.
Health and safety	There are no health and safety risks to this activity.
Layout	Start the session with a playful child (or even a young baby that needs distraction) and remove socks to expose bare toes.
The role of the key person	Singing 'This little piggy went to market' take your time over each of the actions and gently wiggle or tickle the child's toes in turn. Repeat the rhyme with both feet, making sure that the experience is enjoyable and tactile throughout. After a while the young baby will learn to anticipate your actions, so prolonging each before moving on to the next will extend the young babies' enjoyment.
Note	Note the novel ways young babies find out more about themselves and their environment as they become more mobile.
Questions to ask/ suggested interactions	• Can you feel that tickling your little toes? • Shall we do that with the other foot?
Comments	The same fun and enjoyment can be shared with other tactile songs such as 'Tommy Thumb', 'Heads and shoulders, knees and toes' and in older babies 'Wind the bobbin up'.

Creative Development

Creative Development
Being Creative – Responding to Experiences ... (22 – 36 months)   Code: CD 1

Development matters	Play and practical support
Seek to make sense of what they see, hear, smell, touch and feel.	A collection of everyday objects such as wooden pegs, spoons, pans, corks, cones and boxes can be explored alone or shared with adults or other children.

Sample activity	Junk modelling.
Resources	A large selection of different objects. Glue, sticky tape, staples (with adult supervision) and other fixings. Paint in different forms. Aprons.
Health and safety	Ensure that objects are not in danger of transmitting nut or other food allergies. Other food items must be thoroughly washed before use. Use of staples and sticky tape should be supervised.
Layout	Try to collect the goods in boxes that the children can root around in, ensuring that small things do not get lost at the bottom. Set the boxes out in one area, with the fixings in another and paint in another area.
The role of the key person	If the children are unfamiliar with this type of activity, start with a strange or interesting looking piece and ask one of your group: 'What can we make with this?' or 'What does this look like?' to get the ball rolling. Try not to direct the building, but offer help and support with fixings or if a child appears to be frustrated because paint won't stick to the washing-up bottle. Try to ensure that there is a long time available for this session to allow children plenty of time to finish their piece. Put it somewhere safe to dry and display it well once completed.
Note	Watch how children with a specific sensory impairment use other senses in order to enjoy experiences.
Questions to ask/ suggested interactions	• What does this look like? • What can we turn this into? • Would you like me to help you with that?
Comments	Be aware of the frustrations of junk modelling before starting this session, and be prepared. PVA is great, but won't stick plastic to plastic easily so be prepared to offer alternatives. Take care not to use food packaging that may have contained nuts or nut derivatives.

Creative Development

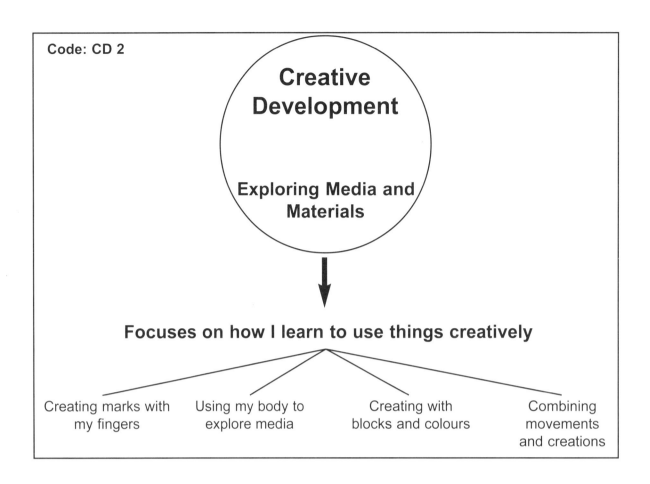

Code: CD 2

Creative Development

Exploring Media and Materials

Focuses on how I learn to use things creatively

Creating marks with my fingers

Using my body to explore media

Creating with blocks and colours

Combining movements and creations

Development Matters

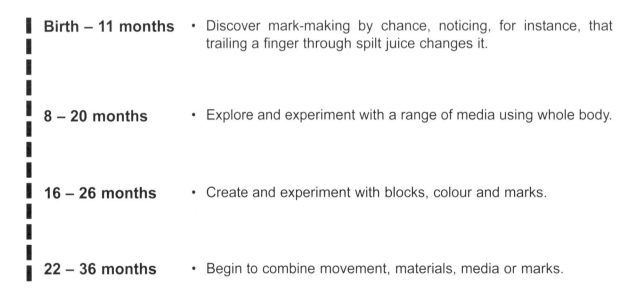

Birth – 11 months
- Discover mark-making by chance, noticing, for instance, that trailing a finger through spilt juice changes it.

8 – 20 months
- Explore and experiment with a range of media using whole body.

16 – 26 months
- Create and experiment with blocks, colour and marks.

22 – 36 months
- Begin to combine movement, materials, media or marks.

You will find suggestions for *Look, listen and note*, *Effective practice* and *Planning and resourcing* in the EYFS Practice Guidance.

Creative Development

Creative Development
Exploring Media and Materials (8 – 20 months)

Development matters	Play and practical support
Explore and experiment with a range of media using whole body.	Materials such as finger paint, PVA glue and wet play give babies the opportunity to delight in sensory exploration and mess-making.

Sample activity	Making a tactile collage.
Resources	Heavyweight card from inside cereal boxes etc to stick your collage materials to. A variety of tubs containing different types of collage materials such as shredded paper, cornflakes, pasta shapes including long sticks of spaghetti, different coloured tiny circles from hole punching, scented sticks of rosemary or sage from the garden etc. PVA glue in a flat open tray. Big aprons.
Health and safety	Ensure that products used do not present a risk of allergic reaction. PVA should be safe for use, but may present problems if fingers are sucked etc.
Layout	Sit your child securely at the table in front of their piece of card which has been taped to the table, with the tub of PVA to their preferred side and tubs of collage materials around the edge.
The role of the key person	Encourage the child to spread the PVA over the card using their whole hand, observing how they react when the glue starts sticking to things. Depending on this reaction you may wish to remove the PVA and wipe their hands before offering them the tubs of collage materials, or you may prefer to leave them to it. Explain/show her that you want her to stick things onto the card, but then take a step back and leave her to attempt it herself. Take care to intervene if she is distressed by things sticking to her hands rather than the paper, wiping her hand if this is distracting her from the activity.
Note	Observe the movements and sounds babies make as they explore materials such as paint, dough, glue and the space around them.
Questions to ask/ suggested interactions	• Can you put lots of this sticky glue onto the paper? • What shall we stick on first? • Would you like me to wipe those sticky fingers?
Comments	Not all children will feel comfortable with this level of mess, so take care to introduce this gradually for those you feel may not like it.

Creative Development

Creative Development
Exploring Media and Materials (22 – 36 months)

Development matters	Play and practical support
Begin to combine movement, materials, media or marks.	Create spaces and opportunities for quiet and noisy play, using a range of materials.

Sample activity	Fabric play.
Resources	A wide selection of different fabrics in different lengths and sizes. Remember to include different textures such as PVC, netting, voile and sari or curtain materials. Add to this a selection of shoes, hats, bags etc.
Health and safety	Close supervision is necessary to ensure there is no risk of strangulation from some of the fabrics such as scarves.
Layout	Start this session by draping the different selections over a chair and spreading the chairs around the space you have available.
The role of the key person	There should be little instruction required before the children are creatively involved in this session. Watch as they wrap themselves in different fabrics and match them with shoes to create a complete image. Make suggestions to those children who seem a little lost for a starting point, such as: 'If we choose this shiny material and those silver wellies, we could pretend to be an astronaut.' Provide help to those struggling with extra long pieces of fabric and, of course, watch to make sure that fabrics do not become tightly wrapped around necks.
Note	Listen to the words children use in their imaginative play and note the learning they are displaying.
Questions to ask/ suggested interactions	• What do you think we can do with this rubbery piece of material? • Why not try teaming it up with these wellies and this hat and becoming a fisherman?
Comments	Providing as many different types of hats, bags, shoes, necklaces and other props will extend or alter this activity significantly. Try leaving some of the pieces in the dressing up box, but keeping some of them aside to make this session different from just dressing up.

Creative Development

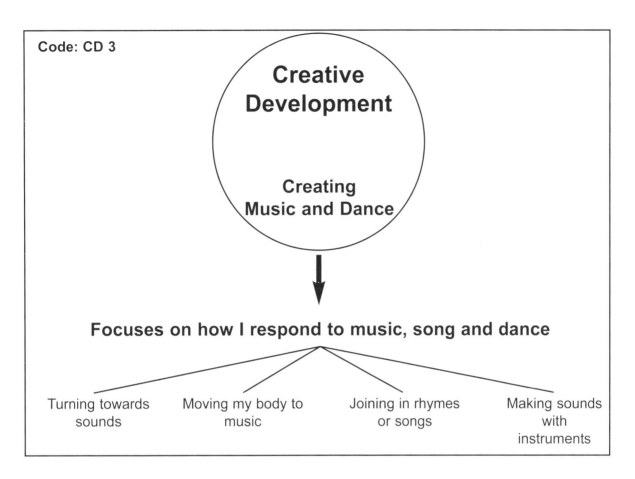

Code: CD 3

Creative Development

Creating Music and Dance

Focuses on how I respond to music, song and dance

| Turning towards sounds | Moving my body to music | Joining in rhymes or songs | Making sounds with instruments |

Development Matters

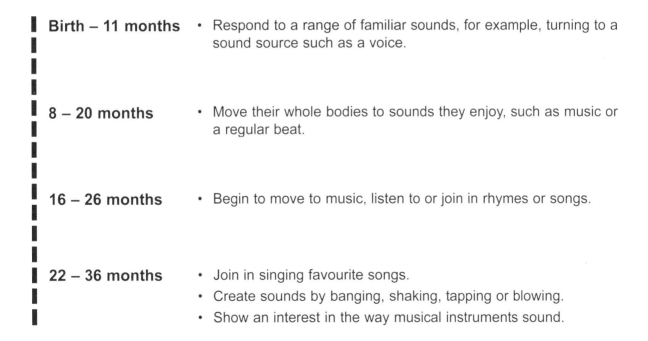

Birth – 11 months
- Respond to a range of familiar sounds, for example, turning to a sound source such as a voice.

8 – 20 months
- Move their whole bodies to sounds they enjoy, such as music or a regular beat.

16 – 26 months
- Begin to move to music, listen to or join in rhymes or songs.

22 – 36 months
- Join in singing favourite songs.
- Create sounds by banging, shaking, tapping or blowing.
- Show an interest in the way musical instruments sound.

You will find suggestions for *Look, listen and note*, *Effective practice* and *Planning and resourcing* in the EYFS Practice Guidance.

Creative Development

Creative Development
Creating Music and Dance (16 – 26 months)

Development matters	Play and practical support
Begin to move to music, listen to or join in rhymes or songs.	Collaborative games and communal sharing times encourage a young child to join in.

Sample activity	**'I am the music man'.**
Resources	A selection of musical instruments so that each child participating has a different piece. It may help for you to have one of each in front of you to use alongside the children.
Health and safety	Ensure that musical instruments used are appropriate to the children's ages.
Layout	Sit in a circle with the musical instruments in front of each participant.
The role of the key person	Sing the tune and encourage all of the children to join in without using their instruments. When it comes to naming the first instrument, choose the instrument that you have given to the first child on your left. Invite him (and only him if you can) to join in with that section of the song while all of the other children sing. If the child is nervous or unsure, pick up your instrument and encourage him to play along with you. Move around the circle in this way until all of the children have had a go on their own, encouraging them to place their instrument on the floor in front of them when it is not their turn. As the last child in the group has completed her turn, make the last verse for a full orchestra and encourage everybody to join in.
Note	Note how you prepare for and resource playful activities for young children to engage in independently.
Questions to ask/ suggested interactions	• Who might be next? • Who has the tambourine? • Can we all clap our hands while John beats his drum?
Comments	Remember to keep this group of children small so that it does not seem like forever that the children have instruments, but must leave them on the floor. Finish the session with a big parade around the room/carpet playing our instruments as loudly as we can.

Creative Development

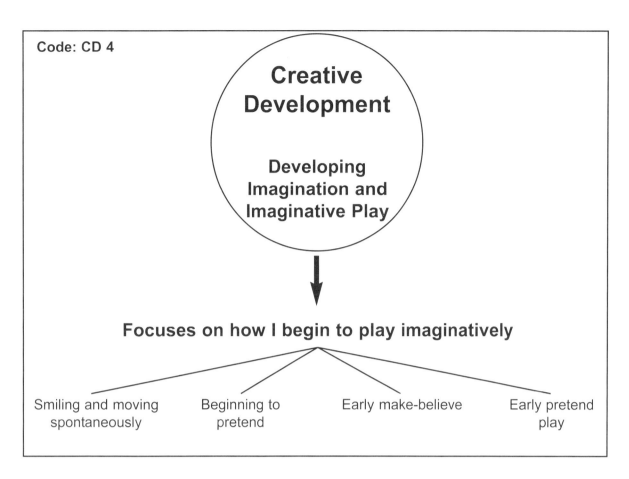

Code: CD 4

Creative Development

Developing Imagination and Imaginative Play

Focuses on how I begin to play imaginatively

Smiling and moving spontaneously

Beginning to pretend

Early make-believe

Early pretend play

Development Matters

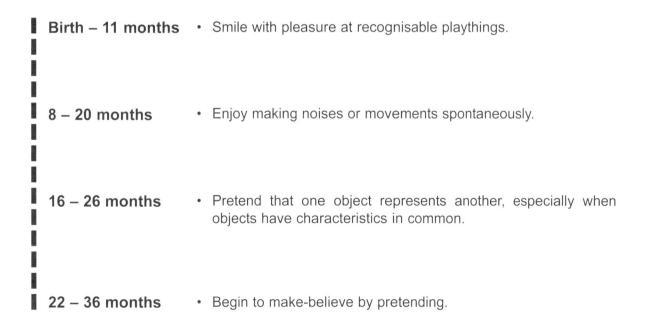

Birth – 11 months
- Smile with pleasure at recognisable playthings.

8 – 20 months
- Enjoy making noises or movements spontaneously.

16 – 26 months
- Pretend that one object represents another, especially when objects have characteristics in common.

22 – 36 months
- Begin to make-believe by pretending.

You will find suggestions for *Look, listen and note*, *Effective practice* and *Planning and resourcing* in the EYFS Practice Guidance.

Creative Development

Creative Development
Developing Imagination & Imaginative Play (Birth – 11 months)   Code: CD 4

Development matters	Play and practical support
Smile with pleasure at recognisable playthings.	A playful adult is a valuable play resource for a young baby. Even sticking out your tongue, wiggling your fingers and tickling is an important game for them. Share a smiling game together.

Sample activity	Copycats.
Resources	Anything that is at hand, but the game is still very enjoyable with just a young baby and a playful adult.
Health and safety	There are no health and safety risks to this activity.
Layout	Wherever you happen to be, but with a good view of each other.
The role of the key person	Catch the eye of a watching young baby and smile. If the young baby smiles back, change your facial expression and watch as the young baby responds. Return to a smile to confirm that the young baby is still willing to play. Include sad expressions, big belly laughs, wrinkling your nose, pulling out your tongue, even covering your face with your hands or a nearby blanket. Keep returning to that first smile until you feel that the young baby is losing interest before closing your session.
Note	Note the situations in which young babies mimic their key person's facial expressions, movements and sounds.
Questions to ask/ suggested interactions	• Can you stick your tongue out? • Can you wiggle your tongue about too?
Comments	This is obviously a game that children of all ages will enjoy, but remember to tailor your copycat images to the baby you are playing with. Complex expressions or stringing too many different actions together before returning to smile are likely to frustrate even the youngest baby.

Creative Development

Creative Development
Developing Imagination & Imaginative Play (8 – 20 months)

Development matters	Play and practical support
Enjoy making noises or movements spontaneously.	Provide varied resources to anticipate what babies and children might need to explore, vocalise and move.

Sample activity	Dressing up.
Resources	A selection of items that the babies can use without adult intervention, such as scarves, hats, bags, ties, shawls. Set alongside it a selection of domestic items such as a telephone, dolls' prams and cots. A selection of dolls or teddies.
Health and safety	Ensure that scarves etc. are carefully watched to ensure no risk of strangulation.
Layout	Arrange the objects so that some are laid out over the chair or cushions, but some remain in the box to encourage exploration.
The role of the key person	Watch to see the babies select items that they can use to represent things from home. Try not to intervene, but if play starts a little slowly you could receive a phone call from Mum and pass it on, or use a scarf to wrap the baby in. Watch how the babies use the items provided, trying to vary items on each occasion.
Note	Observe the sounds they make and how they interact with the resources.
Questions to ask/ suggested interactions	• Is that Laura's mum? Would you like to speak to her? • Why don't we take the babies for a walk in our prams? • Who wears something like this that we know?
Comments	Try to avoid clothing that babies need help to put on, although for older children in this age group the additional challenge will be welcome.

Creative Development

Creative Development
Developing Imagination & Imaginative Play (16 – 26 months)

Code: CD 4

Development matters	Play and practical support
Pretend that one object represents another, especially when objects have characteristics in common.	Young children enjoy playing with real things. Telephones, pans and brushes provide a link with home and lead to imitative and imaginative play.

Sample activity	Role play in the home corner.
Resources	A selection of props to make the home corner realistic. Provide equipment from a variety of cultural settings to ensure that all children have something familiar as well as something to explore.
Health and safety	Care should be taken to ensure that all items included present no risks to children in unsupervised play.
Layout	A home space that is clearly defined, ensuring that a real sense of privacy can be achieved wherever possible.
The role of the key person	The hardest part about role play for the key person is being close enough to observe without intruding, yet being near enough to offer support if requested. Watch carefully to ensure that any intervention on your behalf is *really* necessary. Aim to keep your participation to a minimum.
Note	Look at the kinds of props and materials young children use imaginatively – note anything you might add.
Questions to ask/ suggested interactions	• Try not to ask any questions during the activity, but there may be questions prompted by the things you observed.
Comments	Take care to provide a realistic selection of equipment for this activity. Pots and pans and other cooking utensils may be borrowed from homes if necessary.

Creative Development

Area of Learning: Creative Development		
Focus:	**Age Range:**	Code: CD _____

Development matters	Play and practical support

Sample activity	
Resources	
Health and safety	
Layout	
The role of the key person	
Note	
Questions to ask/ suggested interactions	• •
Comments	

Ⓟ

Completed by: **Date:**

Creative Development
(0–36 months)

Date of activity:	Supervised by:
Children involved:	
Comments	

Date of activity:	Supervised by:
Children involved:	
Comments	

Date of activity:	Supervised by:
Children involved:	
Comments	

Ⓟ

Case studies

Case study

A day in the life of Jamie Jones, aged five months

Time	Activity	Focus
9:10	Jamie arrives at nursery with his mum who is running late for a meeting. Sensing the need for urgency, Jamie's key person Rachel stops what she is doing and immediately goes over to help. She helps Mum take Jamie's coat and hat off, asking how he has been over the weekend. Taking Jamie from his mum, Rachel gives Jamie a big hug and encourages him to wave goodbye. The rest of the group are sitting down for a snack and although Jamie has had his breakfast at home, Rachel pulls up a high chair and sits him with the rest of the group. She gives him a small piece of rusk to chew on so that he doesn't feel left out.	PSED 2 PSED 3
9:30	As the snack is tidied away Rachel moves Jamie and a couple of other young babies to sit propped up by cushions and bouncer chairs in a small circle. She selects a CD and sits herself among the group. Singing along with the music she makes eye contact with the babies in her group in turn, taking their hands and encouraging them to join in.	CLL 3 CD 3
10:00	Another child in Rachel's group becomes upset so she settles Jamie on a comfortable mat underneath a play gym and he happily kicks out to make the mobile pieces dance. After a while Jamie begins to laugh to himself and Sarah who is sitting nearby joins in and asks him what he is laughing at. He responds to her contact and struggles to turn himself more in Sarah's direction. Kicking faster in response he is happy to chat with Sarah from a distance now that he has a better view. Sarah deliberately moves out of Jamie's vision, quickly regaining eye contact saying 'Boo!' Jamie enjoys the game so Sarah continues for a little while until he is distracted and looks away.	PD 1 PSRN 2
10:30	Rachel has a painting session planned with some of her group, but Jamie will not be joining in today. Before starting painting she settles Jamie in his favourite inflatable play nest and fills the nest with light plastic balls from the ball pool. He is happy to paddle his fingers around in the balls for quite some time, tasting some as he goes. Occasionally Rachel replaces balls that he has inadvertently thrown out.	CD 2
11:15	Nearly time for lunch so Rachel tidies away her painting activity and prepares to get Jamie's nappy changed. Talking to him while tidying away the last few pieces, he is waiting for her with arms and legs waving as she picks him up and takes him into the nappy change. Jamie needs a big clean-up before his new nappy goes on so Rachel talks to him constantly throughout. Tickling his tummy, his toes and chubby knees, Jamie is kept well entertained.	PSED 5

A day in the life of Jamie Jones, aged 5 months continued

Time	Activity	Focus
11:45	Lunch is ready so Rachel spoon-feeds Jamie and Holly, talking to them throughout. Holly is more impatient for her lunch than Jamie, but Rachel responds to Jamie's smacking his lips for more with a laugh. After finishing lunch Jamie is ready for his bottle, so Rachel takes him out of his high chair and sits comfortably cuddling Jamie while he drinks from his bottle. Although he is tired, Rachel encourages Jamie to help her hold his bottle. Towards the end of his bottle Jamie is falling asleep so Rachel wipes his face clean with his bib and wraps him in a sheet before lying him down on the floor cushion. She sits with him for a few short minutes until he falls asleep.	**KUW 4** **PSED 2**
1:15	Jamie wakes up before most of the other children and is waving his arms to attract somebody. Sarah picks him up and sits him on her knee. Talking to him, he is struggling to see her face from his angle, so she turns him around and balances him on the end of her knees. She bounces him up and down gently and mimics his facial expressions for quite some time. As other children wake gradually, Sarah sits them in their favourite chairs and cushions in a circle and moves down to join them on the floor, offering each of the young babies a choice from a selection of fabric and board books in her hands for them to enjoy.	**CLL 1**
2:00	The activity planned for this afternoon is shredded paper play. The older children have a huge pile of shredded paper to run or crawl through, but Rachel has saved a small pile to put in Jamie's inflatable ring and he clearly enjoys the whole session. He waves his hands in it, kicks his feet and rubs it into his face, chewing on some of it. Rachel watches him closely and takes the pieces from his mouth before any gets eaten.	**KUW 1**
3:00	Afternoon snack is cream cheese sandwiches in narrow cut fingers so Jamie gets stuck in, squidging his fingers in it and rubbing it into his face as he tastes it. He is clearly enjoying himself when his mum arrives to pick him up. She sits alongside Rachel on the floor waiting for Jamie to finish his snack, giving Mum and Rachel a great opportunity to catch up before he leaves for the day.	**KUW 2**

Case study

A day in the life of Tillie Mint, aged 14 months

Time	Activity	Focus
8:00	Tilly arrives at nursery with her mum who passes over the terry towelling nappies. Tilly is happy to see her key person, Sue, and waves goodbye to Mum easily. Sue helps Tilly build a house with the Mega Blocks.	**PSED 2** **PSRN 3**
8:45	As the babies move through into their own location Tilly is holding Sue's hand, but pulling her through, keen to get to her own room. Sue sits Tilly down at the table, encouraging her to choose her own bib and try to put it on herself, offering a helping hand.	**PD 1** **PSED 5**
9:00	Sheila brings in toast and jam for morning snack, and before the plates are ready Tilly is holding out her hand saying 'Ta' to Sarah who is nearest to the toast.	**CLL 1**
9:30	While other staff tidy away the snack, Sue gets out the guitar that she has brought to nursery and Phil begins to play. Tilly is immediately interested in this and goes over to investigate. Phil shows her how to strum the strings and she is clearly impressed at the sounds she can make. Jeanette gets some more musical instruments out and before long most of the group has joined in. Tilly goes from one instrument to another while she tries them all out and ends up dancing for herself.	**CD 3** **KUW 1**
10:45	After a brief interlude with a different selection of toys, it is time for Tilly's group to visit the Sensory Room with another group. She walks down the corridor by herself, leading the way to get there quicker. Phil is by her side but Tilly prefers not to hold her hand and walk under her own steam. In the Sensory Room, Sue selects the projected images of under the sea and Tilly enjoys following the moving images across the floor for more than 10 minutes, but then instantly dismisses them and runs around the room shouting loudly to hear her own voice. She plays independently with different equipment but stops regularly to check that she is still being watched and laughs when she knows that she has somebody's attention.	**CD 1** **PD 1** **CLL 1** **PSED 2**
11:15	Session over, it is time to walk back to the room for a nappy change and to get ready for lunch. Tilly is not quite so anxious to return and lags behind the group, eventually sitting down on the floor in protest at having to leave. Sue picks her up with a laugh to soften her thunderous expression and Tilly soon softens. Taking her straight into the nappy change Sue can sense that Tilly is getting tired and will need livening up if she is to enjoy dinner and pudding before falling asleep. Sue tickles her tummy and makes her laugh while getting her changed.	**PD 2** **PSED 4** **CD 4**

A day in the life of Tillie Mint, aged 14 months continued

Time	Activity	Focus
11:30	Today's lunch is shepherd's pie with beetroot, which is brought in on plates to cool down. Again Tilly puts on her own bib and tries to get Phil's attention because she is nearest to the lunch. As soon as she has her plate in front of her, Tilly tucks in using her spoon and her fingers to push it on. When all of her group have their lunch Sue sits with them and asks if anybody would like her help. Asking Tilly directly, Tilly refuses to give Sue her spoon to help so Sue lets her get on with it. Watching her closely she offers more help as Tilly gets frustrated that she can't pick anything else up from the bowl. This time she lets Sue help her finish off her shepherd's pie. As her lunch bowl is collected by Jeanette, Tilly objects as Sue wipes her face and hand with a clean cloth in preparation for pudding which arrives almost instantly. Carrot cake is another of Tilly's favourites and she eats it very quickly.	CLL 5 PSED 5 PSED 6
12:10	After another wipe of her face and hands, Tilly is ready for her afternoon nap. Despite numerous attempts by Sue and other key staff, Tilly does not like to go to sleep on the floor cushions or in a cot. Instead she prefers to go to sleep in a buggy so Sue makes her comfortable, wheeling her up and down in the darkened room until she has dropped off. After a short while Tilly can be moved to a floor cushion where she will sleep longer than if she had stayed in the buggy. She is moved carefully, covered with her blanket and given her teddy to hug without her even batting an eyelid.	PSED 1 PSED 2
1:45	Tilly sleeps longer than normal today and wakes in a very good mood. For a little while she is happy playing with the large wooden toys that have been set out but soon spots a group of older children playing outside. Going over to the door she bangs loudly, saying 'Out! Out!' to anybody who will listen.	KUW 1 CLL 1
2:00	Phil brings in a small pile of coats belonging to the older babies and asks Tilly which is her coat. Tilly immediately identifies her coat and gives it to Phil to put on. As soon as her coat is on she stands impatiently at the door again shouting 'Out!' while she waits for the others in her group to have their coats put on. Door opens and she is raring to go. While outside she plays football, runs up and down the patio a great deal and bangs on the windows of other rooms to attract the attention of other children.	CLL 2 PSED 2 PD 3
2:30	Back inside she is ready for something calm so Phil asks her group, 'Would you like a story?' Although she is not in Phil's group Tilly simply takes a seat with the group and enjoys *My Jungle* with the other group. Tilly thoroughly enjoys the book, making verbal comments about the pop-up animals and bright pictures. She remains sitting still while the book is read again, joining in slightly more than the first reading. After this Phil encourages the children to sit with their own books and they all sit happily and read the board books that they are given.	CLL 4 KUW 3

A day in the life of Tillie Mint, aged 14 months continued

Time	Activity	Focus
3:00	Time for afternoon snack and Sheila has arrived with cheese and crackers. Without any instruction Tilly goes over to the table but finds no chairs. Instinctively she goes over to the milk kitchen and bangs at Sue, who she can see through the window. Sue gets the message and helps Tilly to put a chair at the table, asking her: 'Where shall I put it? Do you want to sit by Andrew?' Tilly indicates where she would like to sit by pointing next to Jack and sits on the chair immediately. She enjoys her snack, needing no help at all, and almost helping Jack to finish off his before he spots her.	PSED 6 PSED 3
3:30	After snack time there is a selection of coloured pencils and coloured paper laid out on the tables and Duplo on the floor. Tilly selects a handful of pencils and makes her marks on the paper with all of the pencils at the same time. Looking at her picture she is clearly pleased with her result and gathers a handful of pencils in the other hand too, making her marks on the paper with both hands at the same time. She gets fed up very quickly and drops the pencils, watching as some of them roll off the table and onto the floor. She sits playing with the Duplo, building a tower with Sue until her mum and dad arrive at 4:00.	CLL 6 PD 3
4:00	Sitting playing happily, for a minute or two Tilly is unaware that her parents have arrived. Sue smiles to them but does not draw Tilly's attention to them so that they can watch her play for a while. As soon as they are spotted any building plans are forgotten and she runs as far away as possible so that Dad has to chase her to put her coat on. This gives Mum a chance to ask Sue about her day, and Sue gives her lots of feedback before they leave for the afternoon.	PD 1

Case study

A day in the life of Amelia Smith, aged 20 months

Time	Activity	Focus
9:25	Amelia comes into Blue Room carried by her mum. Mum passes Amelia to Claire who is sitting on the mat about to sing songs with a group of children. Amelia waves happily to her mum and settles comfortably on Claire's knee.	CD 3
9:35	This morning's planner says 'large cars and bikes outside', but it is raining so the room is cleared and other staff members get the cars and bikes out of the shed. As soon as Claire gives the group the go-ahead to play, Amelia charges right the way across the room to get to the shopping trolley before anybody else. Clearly very satisfied with her selection, she steers the trolley over to the home corner and starts putting food items in her trolley before pushing it around the room. As she passes the large black four-wheel drive the driver gets out and without hesitation Amelia lets go of her trolley and gets in. Driving her car around the room, it is really too big for her and she constantly bumps into everybody else, which she seems to find quite funny.	PD 1 KUW 5
10:30	Cars and bikes tidied away, the tables are put back into place and the children will work in their key person groups for the next session. Amelia sits right next to Luke, her key person, and takes the magnets from his hand to stick them onto her magnetic board. She moves them around, taking magnets from other children until she is happy with her picture. Once satisfied with her picture, she moves to the other side of her table and starts on a simple jigsaw. Lee helps Amelia fit one or two pieces in and she completes the jigsaw with lots of praise from Lee. She immediately tips it out and starts again, this time completing it with lots of support but no help from Lee. After completing it a second time, she leaves her table to go and sit by another worker, Justine. Justine is playing with animal figures and her group of children, but is happy for Amelia to join in. Amelia joins in with Justine's group making animal noises.	PSRN 3 CLL 3
11:15	Realising that Amelia's nappy needs to be changed, Justine takes her straight into the nappy change and chats away to Amelia. Amelia answers all of Justine's questions happily.	CLL 1
11:30	Returning from the nappy change, the children are now seated on the mat listening to *Down by the cool of the pool*. Without hesitation Amelia climbs over several children in her way to sit by her friends in the corner. She enjoys the rest of the story, listening and repeating words as the story requires.	CLL 2 CLL 4

A day in the life of Amelia Smith, aged 20 months continued

Time	Activity	Focus
11:45	Lunchtime. Amelia sits down for dinner with her group of friends and waits as her soup is brought to her. Holding her hand out for the crusty bread, she discards her spoon and, dipping her bread into the soup, tucks in. As the bread is finished, she happily picks up her spoon and very competently empties her bowl. Luke asks her if she would like any more, she nods in response and a little more soup is ladled into her bowl. Again she finishes this easily. Shrove Tuesday means pancakes for pudding and Amelia joins in as the children cheer when the pancakes are brought into the room. With her plate in front of her, she does not even attempt to eat the pancakes but uses her spoon to scoop up the cream that accompanies them.	PSED 5 PSED 6
12:15	After lunch Amelia goes with her group to the bathroom to have her face and hands washed. She is given a warm facecloth to wash her own face and does quite a good job. Praising her for a good job, Luke can see a spot she has missed so takes her facecloth and finishes it off for her. He then gives Amelia her toothbrush with toothpaste already on and she moves nearer to the sink and brushes her teeth using appropriate actions.	PSED 5
12:30	Returning to her room, Amelia goes straight over to her floor cushion and lies down to go to sleep. Stella covers her with a blanket and without any additional support, Amelia goes straight off to sleep.	PD 2
1:45	Amelia wakes on her own, lies on her cushion for a little while watching everything that goes on. After a while she gets herself up and goes to join Phil who is reading a story to a group of children.	CLL 4
2:00	Lights on, curtains are opened and the children are offered a new selection of toys for the afternoon. Amelia chooses the sand tray and immediately begins to fill a bucket with sand using a spade. She works slowly and carefully, attempting to build a sandcastle each time the bucket is full. Sometimes it works, sometimes it doesn't but she seems to be enjoying the whole activity.	KUW 1
2:20	After a while Amelia leaves the sand and selects the home corner. She chooses a specific doll and wraps it in a blanket and cuddles it like a baby. Holding the baby carefully, she starts to prepare dinner at the cooker. Caitlin decides to play in the home corner too. Amelia makes room for her and the two girls play happily side by side, but without conversation.	CD 4 KUW 6
2:45	Circle time. Lee is talking to the children about behaviour and about how good everybody has been at playing happily today. He gives out stickers to children, allowing Amelia to select which sticker she would like. As she sits down, Amelia sees the door open and her dad arrive to pick her up. She immediately runs over to him and hugs his legs. Excited at going home, she shouts 'Bye' to all her friends and they shout in return.	PSED 4 PSED 6

Case study

A day in the life of Max Miller, aged 32 months

Time	Activity	Focus
08:00	Max is first to arrive at nursery this morning and rushes straight in to Red Room to see who is in. He stops short in his tracks at the sight of no other children and seems confused about what to do next. Catherine can see his indecision and asks him what he'd like to do. Mum pops her head into the room to say goodbye to Max and he runs over to give her a hug, then immediately runs over to Catherine and puts himself on her knee. They sit and play with the dinosaurs on the table for quite some time, until other children arrive for him to run around with.	KUW 1
08:30	It is time for Max's larger group to move through to their own location and Max joins Justine shouting 'Blue Room' to gather his friends together. Without any instruction Max, Emily and Matthew start to put out the mats in the circle corner. Once completed they run around the mats, bumping into each other deliberately and falling over with loud laughs. Justine starts putting chairs around the tables and the same three children run over to help.	PSED 6 PSRN 3
09:00	Snack time arrives and the same three children rush to sit together at the table without any prompts. They sit impatiently at the table waiting for their snacks, fidgeting in their chairs, pushing at the table. Snacks are ready and Phil asks the children to sit sensibly before she gives them out and the three respond as one. Scotch pancakes and a cup of milk is given to each child. Max has finished his before everybody else has had theirs and asks, 'More, please?' holding out his plate to show it is empty. Enjoying his second helping, he drinks his milk in one go and again asks, 'More please?' Phil responds, 'Would you like more milk, Max? Say more milk please, Phil.' Max happily says, 'More milk please, Phil.' She praises him and tops up his cup.	PSED 5 CLL 1 PSRN 1
09:20	It's circle time and all of the children sit together on the mat. Phil gets their attention by asking, 'Who can point to their eyes?' and takes the children through different body parts. Max joins in happily, knowing all of the parts without hesitation. Moving on to nursery rhymes, Max is happy to join in with a selection of five popular rhymes, singing some very loudly.	PSRN 1 CLL 3
09:30	The room is cleared to enable bikes and cars to be brought in from the shed. Max and Matthew play happily with lots of the cars/bikes, sometimes crashing into each other. Max is quite boisterous in his play and is often vigorous in his assertion to get the bike he wants over somebody else. Occasionally children complain, but not very much, and Max succeeds in getting his way on each occasion.	PD 1 PSED 5

A day in the life of Max Miller, aged 32 months continued

Time	Activity	Focus
10:30	The tables are put back into place and the children are encouraged to work in their groups. Max's group have planned to have a circle session with Joe, the nursery persona doll. There have been issues recently where one of the group has been quite domineering and has on occasion bitten in frustration. Phil introduces Joe to the group again and several of the children say, 'Hello, Joe.' Phil tells the group that Joe is a little upset today because one of his friends had just bitten him and he didn't know why. The children are all very sympathetic and Max is keen to give Joe a hug to help him feel better. Max seems concerned about Joe and is confident participating in this session throughout.	PSED 3 CLL 2
11:00	After this important discussion, the group are taken down to the pre-school room for a role play activity. Currently set out as the manager's office, Max selects a black jacket from the rack and hands it to Phil to put on for him. She offers to help him and helps him find the armholes in this adult-sized jacket. He wants the buttons fastened, but makes no attempt to fasten them for himself. As soon as this is done he realises that Emily has beaten him to the manager's chair at her desk and he shoves the chair out of the way. Emily doesn't seem at all bothered and allows Max to share her desk as she continues to 'write' a letter. Max gets himself a pencil and paper and writes alongside Emily. The children play happily, imitating work observed in Helen's office, including photocopying, shredding paper and making phone calls.	PSED 5 CLL 6
11:35	The children are enjoying their play so much Phil lets them play longer than she had planned so the children need to tidy up quite quickly. Max doesn't want to stop so refuses to help tidy up. He deliberately picks up the telephone and makes a call. Emily takes the phone from him and tells him, 'Tidy up Blue Room.'	PSED 4
11:40	Phil quickly takes her group to the bathroom and encourages Max to sit on the potty before changing his nappy. She praises him for having a dry nappy *and* for using his potty and he is very pleased with himself.	PSED 5
12:00	Lunch has already arrived in the room when Max arrives and he goes straight over to the table. He wants to sit next to Matthew, but there is no chair so he picks another chair and goes to put it in the small space next to him. Luke persuades him to put his chair back where he got it from and sit next to Leyleh, which he does very begrudgingly because his dinner has been put in that space. Using his knife and fork Max tucks in, leaving very little and not allowing himself to be distracted by anything until he has finished eating. He asks, 'More, please?' again, but this time it has all gone. He seems to accept this without any difficulty, puts his knife and fork onto his plate and pushes them away from him into the middle of the table. Pudding is brought in and Max manages this without any trouble. This time he is successful asking for more, but he is only allowed one extra helping, despite additional requests.	PSRN 3 PSED 3 PSRN 2

A day in the life of Max Miller, aged 32 months continued

Time	Activity	Focus
12:25	After lunch Max goes in to the bathroom and washes his face very well, although he makes his sleeves wet in the process. Stella praises him for doing a good job and helps him dry his sleeves a little before giving him his toothbrush to brush his own teeth.	PSED 5
12:40	Max is not very keen to sleep, but his mum has asked that he is encouraged to sleep. Stella lies next to Max and another child and encourages them to close their eyes while they listen to her reading a gentle story. Before long they are both asleep.	CLL 4
1:40	Max wakes up when the lights are put back on and sits straight up, gathers his thoughts for a minute or two and then spots the sand tray. He jumps up still rubbing his eyes, goes straight over to the sand where he promptly throws a handful at Josh who is already in there. Phil reminds him of the talk they had earlier about playing nicely with each other and Max smiles cheekily at her. He picks up a spade and the sieve and plays busily, shovelling and sieving sand over items in the tray for quite some time.	KUW 1
2:00	Group time. Max's group are due to spend this session in the sensory room so line up eagerly to go in. Max is at the front of the line walking to the room. He runs ahead and pushes the corridor door open. As the rest of the group catch up, Max has already taken off his shoes without undoing the laces and left them in the middle of the corridor. Once in the room, Phil turns on some light effects and selects a calming CD while asking the children to sit quietly on the mats. She talks to the children about the things they are planning to do and starts by asking the children if they can crawl like a baby, which Max demonstrates immediately. They then move onto other more complex things such as hopping like a kangaroo (which most of the children including Max are unable to do, but enjoy) and slithering like a snake. Max throws himself into the activities wholeheartedly.	PD 1 CD 4
3:00	Snack time, but this time Max does not eat his scone immediately. Not even tasting it, he pushes his plate away and says, 'Don't like.' Not seeming to be bothered, he drinks his milk and waits for a piece of fruit. He selects a piece of banana, eats this and asks for another, which staff are happy to give him.	PD 2
3:30	Sitting on the mat to sing some songs, the children are invited to request songs to sing. Max shouts out, 'Row your boat' and joins in very loudly when the others start to sing. Other children select songs that Max joins in with, but he declines the offer to stand up and sing to everybody else.	CD 3
4:00	It starts to snow unexpectedly so coats on (no time to practise our dressing skills this time) and out. Unfortunately the snow is very light and is not sticking, but Max enjoys running around trying to catch snowflakes. While he is playing, his mum arrives to collect him and is happy to watch him play while chatting to Phil about Max's day. Spotting his mum, Max is in no hurry to go home and smiles happily, but carries on playing.	PD 1

References

DfES (2007) *The Early Years Foundation Stage*. Nottingham: DfES Publications.

Gallow, C. (2007) *Trackers 0-5: Tracking Children's Progress through the Early Years Foundation Stage*. Stafford: QEd Publications.

Mortimer, H. (2008) *Music Makers: Music circle times to include everyone*. Stafford: QEd Publications.